Alfred Dreyfus, L. G. Moreau

The Letters of Captain Dreyfus to His Wife

Alfred Dreyfus, L. G. Moreau

The Letters of Captain Dreyfus to His Wife

ISBN/EAN: 9783337242848

Printed in Europe, USA, Canada, Australia, Japan

Cover: Foto ©ninafisch / pixelio.de

More available books at **www.hansebooks.com**

CAPTAIN ALFRED DREYFUS

Lettres d'un Innocent

THE LETTERS
OF
CAPTAIN DREYFUS
TO HIS WIFE

TRANSLATED

BY L. G. MOREAU

WITH PORTRAITS

NEW YORK AND LONDON
HARPER & BROTHERS PUBLISHERS
1899

Copyright, 1899, by HARPER & BROTHERS.

All rights reserved.

CONTENTS

	PAGE
INTRODUCTION, BY WALTER LITTLEFIELD	vii

LETTERS OF CAPTAIN ALFRED DREYFUS:

    I. FROM THE PRISON DU CHERCHE-MIDI 1

    II. FROM THE PRISON OF LA SANTÉ 30

    III. FROM SAINT-MARTIN DE RÉ 56

    IV. FROM ÎLES DU SALUT 79

APPENDIX:

    I. LATER LETTERS FROM CAPTAIN ALFRED DREYFUS TO HIS FAMILY 227

    II. A LETTER TO HIS COUNSEL 232

ILLUSTRATIONS

CAPTAIN ALFRED DREYFUS . . . . *Frontispiece*

CAPTAIN ALFRED DREYFUS . . . . *Facing p.* 48
    From a photograph taken on the occasion of his degradation

MADAME ALFRED DREYFUS AND HER CHILDREN .   "   176

DREYFUS, THE MAN

BY WALTER LITTLEFIELD
Author of "The Truth About Dreyfus"

In cases of high treason no less than in violations of the criminal code the personal character of the accused has always had great weight with French judges. In attempting to prove that Captain Alfred Dreyfus carried on treasonable negotiations with a foreign power, M. d'Ormescheville, in his Acte d'Accusation or indictment, laid great stress on the information collected from the municipal police tending to show that the prisoner was an habitual wrong-doer. The supposition that as an Alsatian he might have entered the French army and remained there with the patriotic and unselfish desire to serve Germany is treated with secondary importance. It was the intention of the officer who served as Juge d'Instruction to show that Dreyfus was criminally corrupt, and hence was quite capable of being a traitor. Not only did the semi-official press of Paris, in the winter of 1894-95, dwell upon those acts that seemed intimately connected with the alleged treason, but they delved into his domestic life. With diabolical frankness and in a network of specious details they branded him profligate as well as traitor. The Acte d'Accusation charges him with being a gambler and libertine, unmindful of the well-being of his family, faithless to his wife.

INTRODUCTION

For many weeks this most infamous campaign was kept up in the columns of *L'Echo de Paris, Le Petit Journal, Le Gaulois, La Libre Parole,* and *L'Intransigeant.* So varied in character and so ingenious in conception were these libellous tales, that it became impossible for the friends of the condemned man to make an adequate defense. Dreyfus's counsel, Maître Demange, heard the stories, and could do nothing. The verdict of the court-martial closed the door to legal redress. The devoted wife of Dreyfus at first attempted to reply to them in *Le Figaro.* Parisians laughed at her *naïveté.* She was not the only deceived wife in the world, they said. At length, wearied of the unequal combat—one woman against a horde of anti-Semitic vilifiers—she gave to the world a volume of letters written by her husband to herself. It was her desire simply to show him as he was, to rehabilitate the prisoner as a husband and a father in the eyes of Frenchmen. But " Les Lettres d'un Innocent " have done more than this. To the women of France, at least, they have established the innocence of the man. No one can read these letters without being struck by the absolute sincerity of the writer; by his love for his wife and his family, and for his country; by his devotion to duty and to the traditions of the army whose heads had so remorselessly sacrificed him; by the utter hopelessness of his position. When, in the papers of January 6, 1895, the story of his dramatic degradation was published to the world, the French people pretended to see in his proud, fearless demeanor, as his uniform was stripped of insignia and his sword broken before him, a criminal stoicism that would have been impossible in an innocent man. Many English and American readers recognized simply the

INTRODUCTION

final desperate appeal of an entirely innocent man. The sentiment that was then aroused outside of France will be emphasized by "Les Lettres d'un Innocent." Although not destined to have the judicial and logical weight of the testimony before the Cour de Cassation, they have a sympathetic and persuasive significance that is eminently human. The evidence before the Court proves that Dreyfus did not write the *bordereau*. The letters convince one that he was incapable of treason.

The reader who expects to find in the epistles before us arguments tending to prove the innocence of the writer will be disappointed. Even if the prisoner actually attempted defense it was not allowed to pass the censor. Only a persistent declaration of innocence will be found here—a declaration that is repeated with awful and tragic monotony until it smites the ear like the wail of an innocent soul in Dante's "Inferno."

As has been said, the conditions under which these letters were written forbade the author to indulge in details concerning the circumstances of his awful fate. Hence, for a fuller appreciation and a better understanding of the emotions that moved the writer at given periods, the following data must constantly be borne in mind: Dreyfus was arrested October 15, 1894; his trial by court-martial began December 19 of the same year and ended December 23. The condemned man was publicly degraded January 5, 1895, and on the 9th day of the following February the Chamber passed a law decreeing his place of confinement to be French Guiana, in South America; in March he was transported thither.

The prisoner wrote regularly to his wife until the spring of 1898, when he became a victim of the conditions of his solitary position. In September, 1898, he

INTRODUCTION

bade a final adieu to his wife and children and declared that he would write no more.* He was beset with unconquerable sadness. He complained to his physician, Dr. Veugnon, of Cayenne, of mental exhaustion and insomnia. He was haunted by the "fixed idea" to exculpate himself from the charge of treason. Yet he could only deny and deny.

He knew nothing of what was passing in Paris and in the world at large.

On November 15, 1898, M. Darius, the Procureur Général of Cayenne, entered the room occupied by the prisoner on the Ile du Diable and said to him, "Dreyfus, the Cour de Cassation has decided to revise your case. What have you to say?" Dreyfus seemed like one dazed. The day for which he had so fervently prayed had come at last. Yet, according to his inquisitor, this is what he replied: "I shall say nothing until I am confronted by my accusers in Paris." No further facts were revealed to him, but, under the direction of the authorities in Paris, he was interrogated at given periods. In the mean time he was left a prey to strange conjectures concerning his ultimate fate. On July 3, 1899, he was told that he was to be taken immediately to France to stand trial before a new court-martial at Rennes. He had been a prisoner on the Ile du Diable for more than fifty months.

Alfred Dreyfus, captain in the 14th Artillery, was appointed to the General Staff of the French Army in 1893. He was the first Jew to be so honored. His record at the Chaptal College, at Sainte-Barbe, at the Ecole Polytechnique, at the Ecole d'Application, at the Ecole de Guerre, no less than his service in the 31st

* See Appendix A.

INTRODUCTION

Regiment of Artillery, in the 4th Mounted Battery, and in the 21st Regiment of Artillery, shows that he deserved the distinction. The words of praise that his chiefs then wrote of him are in strange contrast with their later reflections.

For years the Dreyfus family had been identified with large manufacturing interests in Mulhouse, in Alsace. Alfred was one of four brothers. When Germany took possession of the province as one of the results of the Franco-Prussian War, the three younger brothers declared for France, and were obliged to quit German territory; the eldest, who had passed the age of military service, remained behind to look after the business from which the brothers derived their income. It was natural that they should have wished to remain Frenchmen. Had not France emancipated the Jews forty years before they had the privileges of Gentiles under the English law? Since disgrace has fallen upon their family their enduring and emphasized patriotism is somewhat remarkable.

It must not be supposed, on the one hand, that a long period of suspicion was attached to Dreyfus before his melodramatic arrest in the office of du Paty de Clam, or, on the other, that the unfortunate man was the victim of an anti-Semitic plot created for the purpose of ruining him. He was the victim of mistake before he became the martyr of crime. The facts are simply these:

In August, 1894, Commandant Comte Walsin-Esterhazy, who was carrying on treasonable negotiations with the German Embassy in Paris, sent to Lieutenant-Colonel von Schwarzkoppen some notes of information together with a memorandum. This memorandum, or *bordereau*, fell into the hands of a French spy. It was taken to the

INTRODUCTION

Secret Intelligence Department. Its importance as revealing the presence of a traitor who had access to the secrets of the War Office was at once recognized. General Mercier, then Minister of War, placed the investigation in the hands of Commandant du Paty de Clam. Owing to the similarity between the handwriting in the *bordereau* and that of Dreyfus, this officer was suspected of being its author. He was arrested and taken to the military prison of Cherche Midi. In the mean time, du Paty de Clam exhausted every resource to find confirmatory evidence. In this he signally failed. Nevertheless the indictment was drawn up.

Commandant Forzinetti was in charge of Cherche Midi. His first impression of the prisoner as deposed before the Cour de Cassation was as follows:

"I went to Captain Dreyfus. He was terribly excited. I had before me a man bereft of reason, with bloodshot eyes. He had upset everything in his room. I succeeded, after some trouble, in quieting him. I had an intuition that this officer was innocent. He begged me to allow him writing materials, so that he might ask the Minister of War to be heard by him or by one of the general officers of the Ministry. He described to me the details of his arrest, which were neither dignified nor soldierly."

On October 24 Mercier asked Forzinetti what he thought of the prisoner's guilt. This was the reply: "They are evidently on a false scent. This officer is not guilty."

Nearly every day du Paty de Clam visited Dreyfus and tried in every way to force a confession from him.*

This was the position of Minister of War Mercier:

*See Appendix B.

INTRODUCTION

For months a campaign had been carried on against him in the radical press. One fortunate act would vindicate him—the conviction of a traitor. It is impossible that he could have long entertained a belief in the guilt of the prisoner. Yet, having in the first flush of seeming success publicly accused him, he dare not draw back. Already his enemies of the radical and clerical press were accusing him of selling himself to the Jews. "To-morrow," wrote Drumont in *La Libre Parole,* "no doubt they will applaud the Minister of War, when he comes and boasts of the measures which he has taken to save Dreyfus."

Thus the reputation of Mercier, and very possibly the existence of the Cabinet, became staked on the conviction of Dreyfus. Dreyfus was convicted. Space will not permit me to state the exact circumstances by which this most stupendous miscarriage of justice was brought about. Suffice to say, that during a secret deliberation of the court-martial forged evidence was introduced unknown to the prisoner or to his counsel. The criminal code as well as article 101 of the Code de Justice Militaire was grossly violated. It was to cover this illegality and to perpetuate its result that the conspiracy in the General Staff gradually grew into being.

The victim was publicly degraded in the courtyard of the Ecole Militaire, in Paris. The morning was clear and cold. The sunlight shimmered from the gaudy trappings of the Garde Républicaine. "On the stroke of nine from the clock of the Ecole Militaire," wrote a reporter of *L'Autorité,* "General Darras draws his sword and commands, 'Shoulder arms!' The order is repeated before each company. The troops execute the order. Silence follows.

INTRODUCTION

"Hearts cease to beat; all eyes are fixed upon the right-hand corner of the square, where Dreyfus is imprisoned in a low building on the terrace.

"In a moment a small group is seen; it is Alfred Dreyfus in the midst of four artillerymen, accompanied by a lieutenant of the Garde Républicaine and by the commander of the escort. . . .

"Dreyfus walks with a quiet, firm step."

The reporter continues to describe the march across the square to the point in front of the troops where the degradation is to take place. Dreyfus listens in silence while a clerk reads the sentence. General Darras then says, "Dreyfus, you are unworthy to bear arms. In the name of the French people we degrade you."

"Then," continues *L'Autorité*, "Dreyfus is seen to raise both arms, and, head erect, he cries out in a strong voice, in which no tremor is noticed:

"'I am innocent, I swear that I am innocent. Vive la France!'

"And the vast crowd outside answers with a cry of, 'Death to him!'"

The adjutant then begins his work. First cutting from the condemned man's uniform his galloons, cuffs, buttons, all insignia of rank, ending by breaking the sword. During the ceremony Dreyfus several times raises his voice:

"On the heads of my wife and children I swear that I am innocent. I swear it. Vive la France!"

The reporter of *L'Autorité* seems deeply moved, for he adds:

"It is over at last, but the seconds have been as centuries. We had never before felt pangs of anguish so keen. And afresh, clear, and without any touch of emotion, is heard the voice of the condemned man in a loud tone, crying:

"'You degrade an innocent man!'"

The prisoner is then obliged to pass before the line of soldiers. As he approaches the railing the civilian crowd gets a better view of him and yells, "Death to him!"

When he arrives before a group of reporters he pauses and says, "Tell the people of France that I am innocent."

They mock him, however, crying, "Dastard! Traitor! Judas! Vile Jew!"

He passes on and comes to a group of officers of the General Staff, his late colleagues. Here again he pauses, and says, "Gentlemen, you know I am innocent."

But they yell at him as did the reporters. He surveys them closely through his pincenez and says calmly, "You're a set of cowards." There is utter contempt in his voice. At length the direful march is ended. Dreyfus enters a van and is driven to the Prison de la Santé.

For nearly four years the world was a blank to him. Of the efforts made to rehabilitate him he knew nothing. He knew not that the real traitor had been discovered. He knew nothing of the heroic Picquart's unselfish martyrdom in the cause of truth and justice. He knew nothing of Zola's melodramatic entrance upon the scene. He knew nothing of the crimes that were committed in the name of *l'honneur de l'armée*. Was it to be wondered at that he should have been overwhelmed when these things were told him at Rennes?

The story of the indignities that he endured, the tortures that he suffered at the Ile du Diable, has been given to the world by his counsels, Maîtres Labori and Demange. It is like a chapter from the dark ages. Once, when it was reported that an attempt would be made to rescue him, this man, consumed with fever and almost bereft of reason, was, by the order of M. Lebon, Minister of the Colonies, chained to his couch, while the lamp that was kept burning over his head attracted hordes of tropical insects. He was told that his wife sought to forget him and desired to marry again. In his despair his jailers thought he might say something that would incriminate him. They were mistaken. He made no confession. There was none to make. He could only yell in their ears, "I am innocent! I am innocent!" When, in early autumn of 1898, he was believed to be dying this message was cabled from Paris to Cayenne: "Embalm him if he dies, and send us his corpse."

But he lived. And he may still live to see in his appalling experience the cause of social revolution in France—a revolution that shall make the rights of the individual paramount to the traditions of the army, to the subtle cravings of the clericals, to the fantastic schemers of the Faubourg St. Germain.

THE LETTERS

LETTERS

OF

AN INNOCENT MAN

PRISON OF CHERCHE-MIDI

Tuesday, 5 December, 1894.

My dear Lucie:

At last I can write a word to you; they have just told me that my trial is set for the 19th of this month. I am refused the right to see you.

I will not tell you all that I have suffered; there are not in the world words strong enough to express it. Do you remember when I used to tell you how happy we were? Everything in life smiled on us. Then all at once a fearful thunderbolt; my brain still is reeling with the shock. For me to be accused of the most monstrous crime that a soldier can commit! Even to-day I feel that I must be the victim of an awful nightmare.

But I hope in God and in justice. In the end the truth must come to light. My conscience is calm and tranquil. It reproaches me with nothing. I have done my duty, never have I turned from it. I have been crushed to the earth, buried in my dark prison; alone with my reeling brain. There have been moments when I have been nearly crazed, ferocious, beside myself, but even in those moments my conscience was on guard—

"Hold up thy head!" it said to me. "Look the world in the face! Strong in thy conscience go straight onward! Rise! The trial is bitter, but it must be undergone!"

I cannot write any longer, for I want this letter to leave to-night.

I embrace you a thousand times, as I love you, as I adore you, my darling Lucie.

A thousand kisses to the children. I dare not say more to you; the tears come to my eyes when I think of them. Write to me soon.

ALFRED.

Give my love to all the family. Tell them that I am to-day what I was yesterday, having but one care, to do my duty.

The Commissary of the Government has informed me that Me. Demange will defend me. I think that I shall see him to-morrow. Write to me to the prison. Your letters, like mine, will pass through the hands of the government commissioner.

Thursday morning, 7 December, 1894.

I am waiting with impatience for a letter from you. You are my hope; you are my consolation; were it not for you life would be a burden. At the bare thought that they could accuse me of a crime so frightful, so monstrous, my whole being trembles; my body revolts against it. To have worked all my life for one thing alone, to avenge my country, to struggle for her against the infamous ravisher who has snatched from us our dear Alsace, and then to be accused of treason against that country—no, my loved one, my mind refuses to comprehend it! Do you remember my telling you how, when I was in Mulhouse, ten years ago, in September, I heard a German band under our windows celebrating the anniversary of Sedan? My grief was such that I wept; I bit the sheets of my bed with rage, and I swore an oath to consecrate all my strength, all my intelligence, to the service of my country against those who thus offered insult to the grief of Alsace.

No, no. I will not speak of it, for I shall go mad, and I must preserve all my reason. Moreover my life has henceforth but one aim: to find the wretch who has betrayed his country; to find the traitor for whom no punishment could be too severe. Oh, dear France, thou that I love with all my soul, with all my heart! thou to whom I have consecrated all my strength, all my intelligence, how couldst thou accuse me of a crime so horrible! I will not write upon this subject, my darling; for spasms take me by the throat. No man has ever borne the martyrdom that I endure. No physical suffering can be compared to the mental agony that I feel when my thoughts turn to this accusation. If I had not my honor to defend, I assure you that I should prefer death; at least, death would be forgetfulness. Write to me soon. My love to all.

December, 1894.

My good Darling:

Thanks for your long letter of yesterday. I have never doubted your adorable devotion, your great heart.

It is most of all of you that I think in these dark days; I think of your sadness, the grief that you must feel; and in this thought lies my only weakness.

As for me, fear nothing. If I have suffered deeply I have never wavered nor bowed my head. The moments of my deepest anguish have been those in which I have thought of you, my good darling, of all our family. I realised your sorrow when you were without news of me. I had time to think of you all, in the long days, in the sleepless nights, alone with my own thoughts. In those hours I had nothing to read; no way to write! I turned like a lion in its cage, trying to work out an enigma that escaped me. But everything in this world is conquered by perseverance and by energy. I swear to you that I shall discover the wretch who committed the act of infamy. Keep up your courage, my good darling, and look the world in the face. You have the right to do so.

Thank every one for the admirable devotion shown in my cause. Embrace our dear children and all the family for me.

A thousand kisses for your own self, from your devoted   ALFRED.

December, 1894.

My good Darling:

Your letter, which I had impatiently awaited, gave me great consolation and at the same time it made me weep, for it brought me the vivid memory of you, my darling.

LETTERS OF AN INNOCENT MAN

I am not perfect; what man can boast of perfection? But I can assure you truthfully that I have always gone straight forward in the way marked out by duty and by honor.

There has been no compromise between me and my conscience. If I have suffered deeply, if I have undergone the most horrible agony that can be imagined, I have at all times been sustained in this awful struggle by my conscience, which stands on guard, rigid, upright, inflexible. My natural reserve, perhaps a haughty reserve, the freedom of my speech and judgment to-day militate against me. I am not supple, nor a trimmer, nor a flatterer. We never visited the people of the world who might be useful to us now; we shut ourselves up in our own home, we were contented to be happy in ourselves.

And to-day I am accused of the most monstrous crime a soldier can commit!

Oh, if I could but hold the wretch who not only has betrayed his country, but who, besides, has tried to make me bear the burden of his infamy, I do not know what suffering I could not invent to make him expiate the agony which he has forced me to undergo! But we must not despair—they must at last find the guilty one. Without that hope we should have to believe that there is no justice in the world.

Bend all your efforts to reveal the truth; and bring to bear upon them all your intellect, if need be all my fortune.

Money is nothing. Our Honor is All! Tell M[*athieu Dreyfus*] that I count upon him for this work. It is not beyond his power. He must find the wretch who has dishonored us, even though he should move Heaven and Earth. I embrace you a thousand times, as I love you. Your devoted

ALFRED.

A thousand kisses for the children.

All my love to all the members of our families; thank them for their devotion to the cause of an innocent man.

Monday, 11 December.

My good Darling:

I have received your letter of yesterday; also the letters from your sister and from Henri. Let us hope that soon justice will be done me and that I shall once more be with you all. With you and with our dear children I shall find the calm that now I need so much.

My heart is deeply wounded; you know that it must be so. To have consecrated all my strength, all my intelligence, to the service of my country, and then to be accused of the most monstrous crime that a soldier can commit—it is fearful!

At the very thought of it my whole being revolts; I tremble with indignation. I ask myself by what miracle I have been kept from going mad. How has my brain resisted such a shock!

I supplicate you, my darling, do not go to my trial. It can do no good for you to impose new sufferings upon yourself; those that you have already borne, with a grandeur of soul and with a heroism of which I am proud, are more than sufficient. Save your strength for our children. We shall need all our united strength to care for each other, to help each other to forget this terrible trial—the most terrible that human strength can bear. Kiss all our good, dear ones for me, until the time comes when I can embrace them for myself. Remember me fondly to all.

I embrace you as I love you.

Your devoted ALFRED.

Tuesday, 12 December, 1894.

My dear Lucie:

Will you be my interpreter to all the members of our two families, to all who have been thoughtful of me at this time? Will you tell them how much I have been touched by their good letters and by the sympathy they have shown me?

I cannot answer them; for what could I tell them? My sufferings? They understand them, and I do not like to complain. Besides that, my brain reels, and my thoughts are at times confused. My soul alone remains unshaken, as steadfast as on that awful day before the monstrous accusation was thrown in my face. My whole being still revolts at the thought of it.

But in the end the truth must be known in spite of everything. We are not living in a century when the light can be hidden. It must be that the whole truth will be known, that my voice will be heard throughout the length and breadth of our dear France—just as my accusation has been heard. It is not only my own honor which I have to defend; it is the honor of all the corps of officers of which I am a part, and a worthy part.

I have received the clothes that you sent me. If you should have a chance, please send me my tippet. I do not need the pelisse. My tippet is in the wardrobe in the antechamber.

Embrace our darlings tenderly for me. I wept over the good letter written by our dear Pierrot. How long the time seems to me until I can embrace him and you all once more!

A thousand kisses for yourself.

Your devoted   ALFRED.

Thursday, 14 December, 1894.

My dear Lucie:

I have received your good letter; also new letters from the family. Thank them all for me. All these proofs of affection and esteem touch me more than I know how to tell you. As for me, I am always the same. When a man's conscience is pure and calm he can bear everything. I am convinced that eventually the truth will be known; that the assurance of my innocence will finally be borne in upon all minds.

At my trial I shall be judged by soldiers as loyal and as honest as myself. They will recognize—I am sure of it—the error that has been committed.

Error, unhappily, is a human thing. Who can say that he never has been deceived?

I am happy over the good news you give me regarding the children. You were right to begin to give P[ierrot] cod-liver oil; the time is propitious. Kiss the little fellow for me. How I long to hold the dear children in my arms!

I hope, with you, that they will end by letting me

once more embrace you. It will be one of the happiest days of my life; it will be a consolation for all the pain I have endured. ALFRED.

Friday, 15 December, 1894.

My dear Lucie:

I have received your good letter, also mamma's. I am grateful for the sentiment she expresses—sentiments I never have doubted, and which, I can say it proudly, I have merited always.

At last the day of my appearance before justice draws near. I am to come to the end of all this moral torture. My confidence is absolute; when the conscience is pure and tranquil then can we present ourselves everywhere, our heads high. I shall be tried by soldiers who will listen to me and understand me. The certainty that I am innocent will enter their hearts as it has always entered the hearts of my friends, of those who have known me intimately.

My whole life has been the best guarantee of my innocence. I will not speak of the infamous and anonymous calumnies that have been circulated against me. They have not touched me; I scorn them. Kiss all our darlings for me and receive for yourself the tender kisses of your devoted husband, ALFRED.

Sunday, 17 December, 1894.

My dear Lucie:

I do not know that this letter will reach you to-day, for the post-offices are closed, but I will not let the day pass without writing you one word. I am happy to know that you are surrounded by all the family; your grief must be less great, for nothing is more sustaining than such love as is being shown to you.

As to me, my darling, do not give way to any feeling of anxiety.

I am ready to appear before my judges; my mind is tranquil. I am ready to face them as I shall one day stand before God, my head high, my conscience pure.

I am happy to know that you are all well; the children also.

Continue to take good care of yourself, my darling; and keep all your courage. It is true that the trial is great, but my courage is not less great.

If I have had moments of horrible depression, if I have borne the weight of the frightful mental torture, of the suspicion which they have cast upon me, my head has never bent beneath it. To-day, as yesterday, I can look the world in the face; I am worthy to command my soldiers. Embrace the dear ones for me; affectionate kisses from your devoted

ALFRED.

Monday, 18 December, 1894.

My dear Lucie:

I received to-day only your good letter of Saturday. I could not send my letter yesterday; the offices were closed and my letter could not have passed out.

How you must suffer, my poor darling! I can imagine it by comparing your suffering to my own, because I cannot see you. But we must know how to bear up, to hold our own against suffering; we must be resigned; we must preserve all dignity of conduct.

Let us show that we are worthy of one another; that trials, even the most cruel, even the most undeserved, cannot beat us down.

When the conscience is clear we can, as you say so truly, bear everything; suffer everything. It is my conscience alone that has enabled me to resist; had it not been for that I should have died of sorrow, or I should be shut up in a mad-house.

Even now I cannot look back to those first days without a shiver of horror. My brain was like a boiling cauldron; at each instant I feared that my reason would leave me.

Do not be worried by the irregularity of my letters; you know that I cannot write as I would like to; but be strong and brave; be careful of your health.

Thanks for all the news you give me of our friends. Tell them that I have often thought of them; of the grief they must feel. It must bind us in a union that nothing can ever break. Our pure, honorable life, all the past of all our kindred, our devotion to France, are the best guarantees of what we are.

I have received two good letters from J. and R.; they have given me great pleasure.

I thank you also for the news you give me of the children. Ah, the poor darlings! What joy it will be to me to be able to embrace them and you, my good darling! But I will not allow myself to think of it; for then everything seems to melt within me.

The bitterness of my heart rises to my lips—and I must preserve all my strength.

Thank M. and my brothers and my sisters and all the

family for what they have done for me. Embrace them for me.

I will stop, for every memory of the happiness I have known among you all revives my grief.

To have sacrificed everything for my Country, to have served her with entire devotion, with all my strength, with all my intelligence, and then to be accused of such a frightful crime—no, no!

Write to me often; write long letters. My best moments are those when I receive news of you all.

A thousand kisses for you and for the children.

Your devoted   ALFRED.

Tuesday, 18 December, 1894.

My good, dear one:

At last I am coming to the end of my sufferings, to the end of my agony. To-morrow I shall appear before my judges, my head high, my soul tranquil. The trial I have undergone, terrible as it has been, has purified my soul. I shall return to you better than I was before. I want to consecrate to you, to my children, to our dear families, all the time I have yet to live.

As I have told you, I have passed through awful crises. I have had moments of furious, actual madness at the thought of being accused of a crime so monstrous.

I am ready to appear before the soldiers as a soldier who has nothing for which to reproach himself. They will see it in my face; they will read my soul; they will know that I am innocent; as all will who know me.

Devoted to my country, to whom I have consecrated all my strength, all my intellect, I have nothing to fear.

Sleep tranquilly then, my darling, and do not give way to any care; think only of our joy when we are once more in each other's arms—to forget so quickly these sad, dark days!

Until we meet—soon, my darling! soon shall I have the joy of embracing you and our good, dear ones.

A thousand kisses while I wait for that happy moment.
ALFRED.

---

23 December, 1894.

My Darling:

I suffer much, but I pity you still more than myself. I know how much you love me. Your heart must bleed. On my side, my adored one, my thought has always been of you night and day.

To be innocent, to have lived a life without a stain, and to be condemned for the most monstrous crime that a soldier can commit! What could be more terrible? It seems to me at times that I am the victim of an awful nightmare.

It is for you alone that I have resisted until to-day; it is for you alone, my adored one, that I have borne my long agony. Will my strength hold out to the end? I cannot tell. No one but you can give me courage. It is only from your love that I can draw it.

At times I hope that God, who has not abandoned me thus far, will end this martyrdom of an innocent man; that He will bring to light the Guilty One.

But shall I be strong enough to hold out until that time?

I have signed my appeal for a revision. I dare not

speak to you of the children; their memory rends my heart. Speak to them of me. May they be your consolation.

My bitterness is such, my heart is so bruised, that I should already have got rid of this sad life if memory of you had not hindered me; if the fear of augmenting your grief had not stayed my arm.

To have had to hear all they said to me, when I knew in my soul and conscience that I had never failed, never committed even the most trivial imprudence, that was the most horrible of mental torture.

I shall try to live for your sake, but I have need of your aid.

Above all else, no matter what may become of me, search for the truth; move Earth and Heaven to discover it; sink in the effort, if need be, all our fortune, to rehabilitate my name, which now is dragged through the mud. No matter what may be the cost, we must wash out the unmerited stain.

I have not the courage to write more. Embrace our dear relations, our children, everyone, for me.

A thousand, thousand kisses. ALFRED.

Try to obtain permission to see me. It seems to me that they cannot refuse it now.

Monday evening, 24 December, 1894.

My Darling:

It is still to you that I write, for you are the only cord that binds me to life. I know well that all my family, all your family, love me and esteem me; but, after all, if I were to disappear, their grief, however great, would fade with the years.

It is for you alone, my poor darling, that I gather strength to struggle. It is the thought of you that stays my arm. How I feel in this hour my love for you! Never has it been so great—so all absorbing. And then a feeble hope sustains me yet a little; it is that we shall be able some day to have my good name restored to me. But, above all, believe me, if I should have strength to struggle to the end of this calvary, it will be for your sake alone, my poor darling; it will be to avoid adding a new chagrin to all those you have already borne. Do all that is humanly possible to get to see me.

I embrace you a thousand times, as I love you.

ALFRED.

In the night between Monday and Tuesday, 24 December, 1894.

My dear Adored one:

I have just received your letter; I hope that you have received mine. Poor darling, how you must suffer, how I pity you! I have wept many tears over your letter. I cannot accept your sacrifice. You must stay there; you must live for the children. Think of them first, before you think of me; it is the poor, little ones who absolutely need you.

My thoughts always lead me back to you.

Me. Demange, who has just been here, has told me how wonderful you are. He has spoken words in your praise to which my heart gave back the echo.

Yes, my darling, you are sublime in your courage and devotion. You are worth more than I. I loved you before with all my heart and soul; to-day I do more—I marvel at you. You are truly one of the noblest women upon the earth. My admiration for you is so great that if I live to drink my cup to the dregs it will be because I have aspired to be worthy of your heroism.

But it will be terrible to submit to that shameful humiliation! I should rather stand before an execution squad. I do not fear death, but the thought of contempt is terrible.

However it may be, I pray you tell them all to lift their heads as I lift mine; to look the world in the face without flinching. Never bow your heads—proclaim my innocence aloud.

Now, my darling, I am going anew to lay my head upon my pillow to think of you.

I kiss you; I press you to my heart.

ALFRED.

Embrace the little ones tenderly for me.

Will you please deposit two hundred francs with the clerk of the prison?

---

25 December, 1894.

My Darling:

I cannot date this letter, for I do not even know what day it is. Is it Tuesday? Is it Wednesday? I do not know. It is always night. As sleep flies my eyelids I arise to write to you.

Sometimes it seems to me that all this has not happened; that I have never left you.

In my hallucinations all that has happened to us

seems to me a bad nightmare; but the awakening is terrible.

I cannot believe in anything but your love and the affection of all of ours.

We must continually search for the guilty one. All means are good. Chance alone will not suffice.

Perhaps I shall succeed in surmounting the horrible terror with which the infamous sentence I am going to bear inspires me. To be an honorable man, to be innocent, and to see my honor torn from me and trampled under foot—oh, it is fearful! it is the worst of sufferings! worse than death!

Oh, if I go to the end it will be for your sake, my dear, adored one, for you are the only thread that binds me to life!

How we loved each other!

To-day more than ever before I know what place you hold in my heart. But, above all, be careful of your own self; think of your health. *You must, at all costs,* for the sake of my children, who have need of you.

Then search in Paris as you did down there for the guilty one. We must try everything; we must leave nothing undone. There are people surely, there must be people, who know the name of the guilty man.

I embrace you.

Alfred.

Wednesday, 2 P. M., 26 December, 1894.

My Darling:

I have just received your two letters and Marie's.

You are sublime, my adored one, and I am amazed

at your courage and your heroism. I loved you before. To-day I kneel before you, for you are a sublime woman. But do not allow yourself to be beaten down, I supplicate you. Think of our children, who have need of you.

It may be that in my desire to be worthy of you, to reach the heights on which you stand, I shall be able to hold out to the end. It is not physical suffering that I fear—that has never been strong enough to break me down; its blows glance off—but the torture of soul, the knowledge that my name is dragged in the mire, the name of a man who is innocent, the name of a man of honor. Cry it aloud, my darling; cry to every one that I am innocent—the victim of terrible fatality.

Shall we ever succeed in discovering the real guilty one? Let us hope it; to lose that hope would be to despair of everything.

I hope to see you soon, and that is my consolation. All the day, all the night, my thoughts fly to you—to you all. I think of the happiness we enjoyed, and I ask myself, even now, by what inexplicable fatality that happiness was broken.

It is the most awful tragedy that it has ever been given me to read, and instead of reading it, I must live it out, alas! Finally, be careful of your own self, my darling. You need all your health, all your physical vigor, if you are to bring to a successful end the task you have so nobly undertaken.

I embrace you and our poor darlings, of whom I dare not think.

A thousand kisses.

ALFRED.

LETTERS OF AN INNOCENT MAN

Wednesday, 4 o'clock, 26 December, 1894.

My Darling:

You ask me what I do all day long.

I think of you; I think of you all. If this consoling thought did not sustain me, if I could not feel through the thick walls of my prison the strengthening breath of your sympathy, I believe that I should lose my hold on reason and that despair would enter my soul. It is your love, it is the affection of you all, that gives me the courage to live on.

Me. Demange has just been here. He stayed some minutes with me. His faith in me is absolute; that also gives me courage.

It is not physical suffering that affrights me—I am able to bear that—but this continual torture of soul, this contempt that is to pursue me everywhere. I, so proud, so sure of my honor, it is that that I find so terrible; that that I shrink from.

Well, my darling, I will not torture your heart any longer; your grief is already great enough.

I embrace you fondly.

ALFRED.

Wednesday, 10 P. M.

I do not sleep, and it is to you that I return. Am I then marked by a fatal seal, that I must drink this cup of bitterness! At this moment I am calm. My soul is strong, and it rises in the silence of the night. How happy we were, my darling! Life smiled on us; fortune, love, adorable children, a united family—Everything! Then came this thunderbolt, fearful, terrible. Buy, I pray of you, playthings for the children, for their New Year's day; tell them that their father sends them. It must not be that these poor souls, just entering upon life, should suffer through our pain.

Oh, my darling, had not I you how gladly would I die! Your love holds me back; it is your love only that makes me strong enough to bear the hatred of a nation.

And the people are right to hate me: they have been told that I am a traitor. Ah, traitor, the horrible word! It breaks my heart.

I . . . traitor! Is it possible that they could accuse me and condemn me for a crime so monstrous!

Cry aloud my innocence; cry it with all the strength of your lungs; cry it upon the house-tops, till the very walls fall.

And hunt out the guilty one. It is he whom we must find.

I embrace you as I love you.

ALFRED.

Thursday, 10 o'clock in the evening, 27 December, 1894.
My dear Lucie:

Your heroism has conquered me. Strong in your love, strong in my conscience and in the immovable support I find in our two families, I feel my courage born again.

I shall struggle therefore to my last breath. I shall struggle to my last drop of blood.

It is not possible that light shall not be some day let in upon this crime. With the feeling that your heart is beating close to mine I shall bear all the martyrdoms, all the humiliations, without bowing my head. The thought of you, my darling, will give me the strength needful. My dear, adored one, women certainly are superior to us; and among women you are of the most beautiful and the most noble!

I always loved you deeply; you know it. To-day I do more—I marvel at and venerate you. You are a holy, a noble, woman. I am proud of you, and I will try to be worthy of you.

Yes, it would be cowardice to desert life. It would be to taint my name—the name of my dear children—to sully that name forever. I realize that to-day; but how could it be otherwise? The blow was cruel; it broke down my courage; it is you who have lifted me up.

Your soul makes mine tremble.

So, leaning one on the other, proud of one another, we shall succeed, by force of will, in clearing our name from dishonor. We shall remove the stain from that honor that has never failed us.

I embrace you as I love you.

ALFRED.

Thursday, 11 o'clock in the evening.

I almost hoped to receive one more word from you this evening. If you could only know with what happiness I receive your letters, with what intoxication I read and re-read them all day long!

Good-night; sleep well, my darling. We will live still for each other.

LETTERS OF AN INNOCENT MAN

Friday, 10 o'clock in the morning, 28 December, 1894.
My dear Lucie:

I have received your good letter dated yesterday at noon. You are right. I must live. I must live for you—for our dear children, whose name I must restore to honor. Whatever may be the terrible tortures of soul I endure, I must resist. I have no right to desert my post.

If I were alone, I should not hesitate; but your name, the name of my family—everything, all we have, is attacked. We must arm with all our courage for the struggle. By the force of our energy, our will, we shall triumph. In the end they shall speak out. Supported, sustained by your unfailing courage, we shall conquer.

Write to me often. You must relieve each other in writing; write to me in turn. Each one of your letters soothes me. It seems to me that I hear you speak—that I hear your dear parents speak.

I embrace you and all your dear family.

A thousand tender kisses to the children.

ALFRED.

Friday, noon.

I received your letter dated Thursday evening, also the good words from Pierrot. Embrace the darling tenderly for me. Give Jeanne a kiss for me. Yes, I must live. I must summon all my energy to wash out the stain which sullies the name of my children. I should be cowardly should I desert my post. I will live; I will!

I embrace you. ALFRED.

LETTERS OF AN INNOCENT MAN

Monday, 31 December, 1894.

My dear Lucie:

I thought a long time last night of my father, of all my family. I do not hide from you that I wept long. But the tears comforted me. Our consolation is the deep affection that unites us all; it is the affection which I find in your family as in my own.

It is impossible, when we are so bound together, when we are upheld by the wonderful devotion shown us by Me. Demange, that we shall not sooner or later discover the truth. I was wrong to wish to desert life. I had not the right to. I will struggle as long as I have a breath of life. In these long days, in these sad nights, my soul is purified and strengthened. My duty is clearly traced. I must leave my children a name pure and stainless.

Let us strive for that, my darling, without a truce, without rest. Let us not be rebuffed by the difficulty of any step, of any attempt. We must try everything.

The books of M. Bayles, which you sent me, are enough for the moment; later I shall need a work with exercises, with corrections on the opposite page; so that I can work by myself.

For the moment I must gather all my strength to meet the horrible humiliation that awaits me. But do not relax a single instant. You may, perhaps, enter upon a course of which I have spoken to Me. Demange this evening. Nothing must be neglected; everything must be tried.

I embrace you as I love you.

ALFRED.

Good kisses to the darlings. I dare not wish you " A

LETTERS OF AN INNOCENT MAN

Happy New Year;" this feast does not accord with our present sorrow.

I have even forgotten to wish your mother a happy birthday. I pray you to repair this forgetfulness; it is excusable under the sad circumstances.

I suppose you have given the children the toys from their father. We must not let these young souls suffer through our sorrows.

I have received the inkstand. I thank you for it.

---

5 o'clock in the evening.

The appeal is rejected, as I might have expected it would be. They have just told me. Ask immediately for permission to see me.

Send me what I asked you for; that is to say, my sabre, my belt, and the valise with my belongings. The cruel and horrible anguish is approaching; I am going to meet it with the dignity of a pure and tranquil conscience. To tell you that I do not suffer would be to lie; but I shall not weaken. I shall be strong. Keep on, for your part, without truce, without rest.

---

1 January, 1895.

My Darling:

It is no longer Sunday. It is the beginning of Monday. The stroke of midnight has just sounded at this moment, as I lighted my candle. I cannot sleep. I would rather rise than toss upon my bed, and what more delicious occupation than to talk with you! When I write it seems that you are near me, as it used to be in those good evenings of my happy memories, when, as I sat at my desk, you would work by my side.

Let us hope—let us hope that happiness shall shine again for us. It is impossible that some day the light of truth shall not make all clear. I know the energetic character of Mathieu; I have learned to appreciate your energy, your profound devotion, I will say your heroism; and I do not doubt the success of your investigations.

You are right to act with calmness, with method. Your progress will be surer.

But I hope that soon I can speak of all this face to face with you.

From this hour the agony is to become still more bitter. First, the humiliating ceremony, then the sufferings which will follow it. I shall bear them calmly, with dignity—be sure of it.

To say that I have not at times moments of violent revolt would be to lie. The injustice is by far too cruel; but I have faith in the future; and I hope to have my recompense.

So I try to think that the time will come when my only care will be to ensure my happiness—the happiness of our dear children.

I have received a charming letter from Marie, which I shall answer one of these days.

Be of good courage always, my darling. Take good care of your health, for you will have need of all your strength; your courage must not betray you in the crucial moment. Good-night and good rest.

I embrace you as I love you.

ALFRED.

LETTERS OF AN INNOCENT MAN

Tuesday, 1 January, 1895.

I have not received a letter from you this morning. I miss it. I have received several others, it is true; but dare I tell you that it is not the same thing? Yesterday, when he left me, Me. Demange hoped to come back and pass some hours with me to-day; but alas! not long after his departure they told me that my appeal had been rejected; this closes my prison door to him; he will not be permitted to visit me any more. He must have been warned this morning. So I shall pass my day alone. What a sad New Year, my darling! But do not let us dwell upon this subject. It will do us no good to weep and groan; that will not open the doors of my prison. On the contrary, we must guard all our physical strength and all our mental energy; we must not relax our struggle for one instant. Let nothing beat you down; do not lose hope. Throw your nets out on all sides; the guilty one will be caught in them at last.

Have you received an answer to your application? I am waiting now with impatience for the moment when I shall hold you in my arms.

Have you bought the toys for the children? Were they pleased? I am thinking always of you and of them. I live only in the thought that some day this frightful nightmare will vanish. It seems impossible that it can be otherwise. We will help overcome it, I promise it to you. I embrace you as I love you.   ALFRED.

Monday, 2 January, 1895, 11 o'clock in the evening.
My Darling:

A new year is beginning. What has it in store for us? Let us hope that it will be better than the year that is just ended. Should it be otherwise, death would be preferable. In this calm, deep night which surrounds me, I think of you all, of you, of our dear children. What a fearful stroke of fate, undeserved and cruel!

Let me give way a little, weep without restraint in your arms. Do not believe because I weep that my courage weakens. I have promised you to live; I shall keep my word. But I must always feel your heart beating close to mine. I must be sustained by your love.

We must have courage. We must have an almost superhuman energy. As for me, I can only summon my whole strength to bear all the tortures which await me.

Good-night and kisses.

ALFRED.

Thursday, noon.

My Darling:

They have informed me that the supreme humiliation is set for the day after to-morrow. I expected it; I was prepared for it; but in spite of that the blow was terrible. I shall stand fast, as I promised you I would. I shall draw the force I still need for that awful day from the deep well of your love, from the affection of you all; from the memory of our dear children; from the supreme hope that some day the truth will come to light; but on every side I must feel the warmth of the affection that you all bear me. I must feel that you are struggling with me. Search always; let there be no truce, no rest.

I hope to see you soon, to gather strength from your loving eyes. Let us sustain each other through everything and against everything.

Your love is necessary to my life; without it the mainspring of my being would be broken.

When I am gone persuade them all that they must not stop their efforts.

Take measures at once, so that you may be able to come to see me on Saturday and the following days at the prison of la Santé. It is there, above all, that I must feel that I am sustained.

Find out also what I asked you yesterday—when I am to leave, how I am to go, etc.

We must be prepared for everything; we must not let ourselves be surprised.

Until the blessed moment, soon to come, when I shall see you, I embrace you. ALFRED.

4:15 P. M.

Since four o'clock my heart has been beating to bursting. You are not yet here, my darling. The seconds seem hours to me. My ear is listening—perhaps they come to call me. I cannot hear; I am waiting.

---

5 o'clock.

I am more calm; the sight of you has helped me. The rapture of having held you in my arms has done me immense good. I could not wait for the moment. I thank you for the joy that you have given me. How I love you, my good darling! Let us hope that some time all this sorrow is to end.

I must husband all my energy.

A thousand kisses more, my darling.
ALFRED.

LETTERS OF AN INNOCENT MAN

Thursday, 11 o'clock in the evening.

My Darling:

The nights are long; it is to you that I turn again and again; it is in your eyes that I look for all my strength. It is in your profound love that I find the courage to live. Not that the struggle makes me afraid, but truly fate is too cruel to me. Could one imagine a situation more awful, more tragic, for an innocent man? Could there be a martyrdom more fraught with sorrow?

Happy is it for me that I have the deep affection with which both our families surround me—that above everything I have your love, which pays me for all my sufferings.

Forgive me if sometimes I complain; do not think that my soul is less valiant because a groan escapes my lips; these cries relieve my heart; and to whom could I cry if not to you, my dear wife?

A thousand kisses for you and for the little ones.

ALFRED.

Wednesday, 5 o'clock.

My Darling:

I wish to write these few words more, so that you may find them to-morrow morning when you awake. Our conversation, even through the bars of the prison, has done me good. My limbs trembled under me when I went down to met you, but I gathered all my strength, so that I should not fall from my emotion. Even now my hand is still trembling; our interview has violently shaken me. If I did not insist that you should stay still longer it was because I was at the end of my strength. I had to hide myself, so that I might weep a little; do not believe because I weep that my soul is less brave or less strong; but my body is somewhat weakened by three months of the prison, without a breath of the outer air. I must have had a robust constitution to have been able to resist all these tortures.

What has done me the most good is that I felt that you were so brave, so valiant, so full of love for me. Let us, my dear wife, continue to command the respect of the world by our attitude and by our courage. As for me, you must have felt that I am decided to face everything. I want my honor, and I shall have it. No obstacle shall stop me.

Kiss the babies for me. A thousand kisses.

ALFRED.

The parlor is to be occupied to-morrow, Thursday, from 1 until 4 o'clock. So you must come either in the morning between 10 and 11 o'clock, or in the afternoon at 4 o'clock. This takes place only Thursdays and Sundays.

IN THE PRISON OF LA SANTE.

5 January, 1895.

I will not tell you what I have suffered to-day. Your grief is great enough already. I will not augment it.

In promising you to live, in promising you to resist until my name is rehabilitated, I have made the greatest sacrifice that a man of deep feeling of heart, an upright man, from whom his honor has been taken, can make. My God, let not my physical strength abandon me! My spirit is unshaken; a conscience that has nothing with which to reproach me upholds me, but I am coming to the end of patience and of my physical strength. After having consecrated all my life to honor, never having deserved reproach, to be here, to have borne the most wounding affront that can be inflicted upon a soldier!

Oh, my darling, do everything in the world to find the guilty one; do not relax your efforts for one instant. That is my only hope in the terrible misfortune which pursues me.

If only I may soon be with you there, and if we may soon be united, you will give me back my strength and my courage. I have need of both. This day's emotions have broken my heart; my cell offers me no consolation.

Picture a little room all bare—four yards and a half long, perhaps—closed by a grated garret window; a pallet standing against the wall—no, I will not tear your heart, my poor darling.

I will tell you later, when we are happy again, what I have suffered to-day, in all my wanderings, surrounded by men who are truly guilty, how my heart has bled. I have asked myself why I was there; what I was doing there. I seemed the victim of an hallucination; but alas! my garments, torn, sullied, brought me back roughly to the truth. The looks of scorn they cast on me told me too well why I was there. Oh, why could not my heart have been opened by a surgeon's knife, so that they might have read the truth! All the brave, good people along my way could have read it: *"This is a man of honor!"* But how easy it is to understand them! In their place I could not have contained my contempt for an officer who I had been told was a traitor. But alas! there is the tragedy. There is a traitor, but it is not I!

Write to me soon; do everything in your power so that I may see you, for my strength is giving way. I need to be upheld; come, so that we may be together once again, that I may find in your heart all the strength I need in this awful hour.

I embrace you as I love you.

Saturday afternoon. ALFRED.

Saturday, 6 o'clock, January, 1895.

In my dark cell, in the tortures of my soul, which refuses to understand why I suffer so, why God so punishes me, it is always to you that I turn, my dear wife, who, in these sad and terrible moments, have shown for me a devotion without boundaries, a love illimitable.

You have been and you are sublime; in my moments of weakness I have been ashamed not to be at the height of your heroism. But this grief must gnaw the best disciplined soul; the grief of seeing so many efforts, so many years of honor, of devotion to one's country, lost because of a machination that seems to belong to the realms of the grotesque, rather than to real life. Sometimes I cannot believe it; but these moments, alas! are rare here, for subjected to the strictest discipline of the prison cell, everything reminds me of the dark reality. Continue to sustain me with your profound love, my darling; aid me in this awful struggle for my honor; let me feel your beautiful soul throbbing close to mine.

When can I see you?

I need affection and consolation in my sorrow.

Alas! I may have the courage of a soldier, but I ask myself have I the heroic soul of the martyr!

A thousand good kisses for you, for our darlings. May these children be your consolation.

A. Dreyfus.

Write to me often and at length. Think that I am here alone from morning until evening, and from evening until morning. Not one sympathetic soul comes to lighten my dark sorrow. I long to be there with you, where I can wait in peace and tranquillity, until they rehabilitate me—until they give me back my honor.

---

7 o'clock, evening, 5 January, 1895.

I have just had a moment of terrible weakness; of tears mingled with sobs; all my body shaken by the fever. It was the reaction from the awful tortures of the day. It had to be—I knew it. But alas! instead of being allowed to sob in your arms, to lean my head upon your breast, my sobs have resounded in the emptiness of my prison. It is finished. Be lifted up, my heart; I concentrate all my energy. Strong in my conscience, pure and unstained, I owe myself to my family, I owe myself to my name. I have not the right to desert. While there remains in me a breath of life I will struggle, hoping that light soon may be let in upon the truth. And do you continue your searches. As for me, the only thing that I ask is to leave here as soon as possible; to find you there; to settle down to our life there, while our friends, our families, are busy here searching for the guilty one, so that we may come back to our dear country, martyrs who have borne the most terrible, the most harrowing, of trials.

LETTERS OF AN INNOCENT MAN

Saturday, 7:30 P. M.

It is the hour when we are obliged to go to bed. What will become of me? What am I going to do when I am in my bed, a straw mattress supported on iron rods. Physical sufferings are nothing—you know that I do not fear them—but my moral tortures are far from being ended. Oh, my darling, what did I do the day I promised you to live! I thought then that my soul was stronger. It is easy to talk of being resigned because the heart is innocent, but it is hard to be so.

Write to me soon, my darling; try to see me. I need to draw new strength from your dear eyes.

A thousand kisses. ALFRED.

Sunday, 5 o'clock, 6 January, 1895.

Forgive me, my adored one, if in my letters yesterday I poured out my grief and made a parade of my torture. I must confide them to some one. What heart is better prepared than yours to receive the overflowing grief of mine? It is your love that gives me courage to live; I must feel the thrill of your love close to my heart. Let us show that we are worthy of each other; that you are a noble, a sublime wife.

Courage, then, my darling. Do not think too much of me; you have other duties to fulfil. You owe yourself to our dear children, to our name, which must be restored to honor. Think, then, of all the noble duties incumbent upon you. They are heavy, but I know that you will be capable of undertaking, of accomplishing them all, if you do not let yourself be beaten down—if you preserve your strength.

You must struggle, therefore, against yourself. Summon all your energy; think only of your duties.

As to me, my darling, your know that I suffered yesterday even more than you can imagine. I shall tell you how much some day, when we are once more happy and united. For the present I hope but one thing. Since I am useless to you here, and since, on the other hand, the search for the guilty man will, I fear, be a long one, I hope to be sent down there soon, and under the best conditions possible to wait there with you until the combined efforts of all our relations shall have been successful. The life of the prison cell is wearing me out, and I ask but one thing, to be sent down there as soon as possible. I was heart-broken this morning because I did not get any letters. Happily, at 2 o'clock, the director of the prison brought me a package of good letters, which gave me much pleasure. They have been the one ray of joy in my wretched cell. Will you please send me my travelling rug, for it is very cold in our cells.

Try to obtain permission to see me as soon as possible.

I embrace you a thousand times.   ALFRED.

Good kisses to the poor darlings.

---

7 o'clock in the evening.

My God, how sorrowful is my soul! What in all my life have I done that I should be thus punished? The wretch who has committed the crime of betraying me, the wretch through whom I am lost, deserves, if there is a God, a terrible chastisement. He deserves to be punished through all he loves. In the name of my poor children I curse him.

LETTERS OF AN INNOCENT MAN

Monday, 5 P. M., 7 January, 1895.

My Darling:

I have borne for your sake, my adored one, for the name which my dear children bear, the most agonizing, the most appalling, of calvaries for a heart that is pure and honorable. I ask myself how I am yet alive. That which sustained me is, above all else, the hope that I shall soon be united to you down there. Then, though innocent as I am, but sustained as I shall be by your profound love, I shall have the patience to await in exile the vindication of my name. There, too, I shall work, I shall be busy. I shall impose silence upon my heart and my brain by force of physical fatigue. But in my prison it would be difficult to live, for my thought always brings me fatally back to my condition.

They have not given me any letter from you to-day; do not be anxious, my darling, if my letters do not reach you regularly. I will write to you every day as long as I am permitted to.

I have been told that I can see you Monday and Friday. Alas! Monday has passed, and I am obliged to wait until Friday. I wait with extreme joy for the moment when I can kiss you; when I can throw myself into your arms. It is in your eyes, in your noble heart, that I find the strength needful to enable me to bear my fearful tortures of soul. I should almost like it better had I some sin upon my conscience; then I should, at least, have something to expiate. But alas! you know, my darling, how honest, how upright, my life has always been.

I will do all I can to live. I will do all I can to resist until the supreme moment when they give back to me the honor of my name.

LETTERS OF AN INNOCENT MAN

But I shall bear the waiting better when you are there, in exile, with me. So, together, proud and worthy of one another, we will, in exile, give proof of the calm of two pure, honest hearts; of two hearts whose thoughts have always all been given to our dear country—France.

Good kisses to our poor darlings. Kisses to all our friends.

I embrace you as I love you.

ALFRED.

---

8 January, 1895.

My Darling:

They have given to me to-day your letters of Sunday, also those sent to me by R., H. and A.

Thank them all. Give them news of me. Pray them to write to me, but tell them that it is impossible for me to answer them all. Not that the time is lacking, alas! but I cannot abuse the time and the kindness of the director of the prison, who is obliged to read all my letters. I am relatively strong in this sense: that I live by hope. But I feel that this situation cannot be prolonged. I have, and this is easy to understand, moments of violent revolt against the injustice of my fate. It is truly terrible to suffer as I have suffered through these long months for a crime of which I am innocent. My brain, after all these shocks, has moments of wandering.

I hope to see Me. Demange this evening and to beg of him to take steps with those who have the power to grant my prayer, so that they will, under conditions which I shall indicate, arrange to have me sent into exile with you, to wait until light is let in upon this crime. As to this last, I have great hope. My efforts must eventually have their reward. But I must have air, hard physical work, your dear society, to steady my brain, which has been shaken by so many shocks. Great God, how little I expected them!

Pray Me. Demange, who has obtained permission to see me, to come as soon as he can, so that I may explain to him the favor asked by an innocent man waiting until complete justice shall be done him.

You ask me also, my darling, what I do from morning until night. I do not want to tell you all my sad reflections. Your grief is great enough, and it is useless to add to it. What I have said above will tell you what at this moment I desire, exile with you in the free air, while I await my vindication.

As to the rest I will tell it all to you by and by, when we are together again and happy.

I will confide one thing to you, however—in the moments of my deepest sadness, in my moments of violent crisis, a star shines all at once, lighting up my brain and beaming upon me. It is your image, my darling, it is your adored image that I hope soon to behold face to face. And with that before me I can wait patiently until they give me back that which I hold dearest in this world—my honor, my honor that has never failed me.

Embrace them all for me. Kisses to the darlings.

I embrace you a thousand times.

ALFRED.

How impatiently I wait for Friday! What a pity that you came to-day at the hour of the director's luncheon; had you come at some other time perhaps they might have permitted you to embrace me.

LETTERS OF AN INNOCENT MAN

Tuesday, 7 o'clock in the evening.

They have just given me a whole package of letters—from Jeanmaire, from your father, from Louise, and from you. Thank them all for writing to me. The letters have made me weep, but they have eased my wounded soul. Answer every one for me.

---

9 January, 1895, Wednesday, 5 o'clock.

My good Darling:

I, also, receive my letters only after a long delay. They have only now given me your letter of Tuesday morning. With it were numerous letters from all the family. What can we do, my darling? We must bow our heads, we must suffer without complaining. Truly, even now, when I think it over, I wonder how I could have had the courage to promise you to live on after my condemnation. That day, that Saturday, is burned into my mind in letters of fire. I have the courage of the soldier who goes forward gladly to meet death face to face; but alas! shall I have the soul of the martyr?

But be tranquil, my darling. I shall force myself to live and to resist until the day of my vindication. I have borne without flinching the anguish of the most wounding affront that can be imposed upon a man of heart who is innocent, whose conscience is pure. My heart has bled; it bleeds still. I live only by the hope that they will give me back my place in the army, the place I won by gallant and meritorious conduct—the *galons* that no act of mine had ever sullied!

And moreover, whatever sufferings may still await me, my heart commands me to live. I must resist; I must resist for the name that is borne by my dear children, for the name of all the family.

But duty is sometimes hard to follow. You speak of my life in this prison—what good can it do to increase your sadness, my darling? Your grief is great enough without my augmenting it by my complaining.

I live by hope, my good darling. I live, because I believe that it is impossible that the truth shall not some day be made clear, because it cannot be that my innocence shall not be some day recognised and proclaimed by this dear France—my country, to whom I have always brought my intelligence and my strength—to whom I would have consecrated all the blood that is in my veins.

I must have patience; I must draw it from the deep well of your love, from the affection of all those who love us, and from the conviction that I shall ultimately be rehabilitated.

A thousand kisses to the darlings.

I embrace you as I love you.

ALFRED.

Your letter tells me that they have refused to permit Me. Demange to see me; I hope, notwithstanding this, that they will soon accord him the permission.

I count the hours until Friday, when I shall see you. Thanks for the good letters I receive from all. Thank them all for me and tell them that one of the best hours in my day is that which I pass in reading my letters. But I am incapable of answering all of them. I can say nothing except that I am resigned and that I expect that the truth will be discovered.

LETTERS OF AN INNOCENT MAN

10 January, 1895, 9 A. M.

Since two o'clock this morning I could not sleep for thinking that to-day I should see you. It seems that even now I hear your sweet voice speaking to me of my dear children, of our dear families, and if I weep I am not ashamed of it, for the martyrdom that I endure is truly cruel for a man who is innocent.

Who is the monster who has thrown the brand of evil, of dishonor, into a brave and honorable family?

If there is such a thing as justice on this earth, there is no punishment too great to be reserved for him, no torture that should not some day be inflicted on him.

But my courage is not weakening. I have painful moments, when my eyes are veiled by the mournful darkness of the present; but I comfort myself by looking forward to the future.

Your devotion is so heroic—you are all making such powerful efforts, it is impossible that the truth shall be forever hidden. Besides that, the truth must be made plain, *it must be;* the will is a powerful lever.

Now, at once, my darling, I am to have the joy of embracing you, of clasping you in my arms. I count the seconds which separate me from that happy moment.

Half-past 3 o'clock, P. M., 10 January, 1895.

The moment is passed, my darling; so quick, so short, that it seems to me I have not told you the twentieth part of what I had to say. How heroic you are, my adored one! How sublime is your self-forgetfulness, your devotion! I can do nothing but wonder at you.

Under the combined influence of your loving sympathy and of your heroic efforts I have not the right to hesitate.

I will suffer, then, I will not murmur, but let me when my heart overflows weep out my anguish on your breast.

The cruelest of all is this—I cannot repeat it too often—it is not the physical suffering that I endure; it is this atmosphere of contempt which surrounds my name—your name, my adored Lucie. You know that I have always been proud, dignified. You know that I have held duty above all else. You can therefore appreciate all that I suffer now. And that is why I wish to live; that is why I cry my innocence to all the world. I will cry it each day until my last breath, while in my body there is one drop of blood.

I shall find in your dear eyes the courage needful for my martyrdom. I shall draw from the memory of my children the strength to resist to the end of my agony.

Bring me your portrait, too. I will place it between the pictures of our darlings, and contemplating those faces, I shall each day, each instant, read my duty.

Embrace all for me.

ALFRED DREYFUS.

Thank your sister Alice for her excellent letter, which has given me a great deal of pleasure. Also give me news of all the members of the family, to whom I cannot write. Tell them that their letters are always welcome.

I embrace you tenderly.

ALFRED.

Half-past 7 in the evening.

I have to-day received no letter from you—no letter from any one. Have they been stopped on the way? However that may be, I have to-day been deprived of the only ray of sunlight which can lighten the darkness of my prison.

P. S. Just now, as I was about to go to bed, they brought me a package of letters, which I am going to devour with delight.

Thursday, 5 o'clock in the evening, 11 January, 1895.

My Darling:

I thank you for your two last letters (one written Tuesday and the other written, I think, Wednesday morning). They have just given them to me. Write to me morning and evening. Although I receive the two letters at the same time, nevertheless I can follow you in my thoughts. I see you in all you do. It seems to me that I am living near to you.

I occupy my time in reading and in writing; in that way I try to calm the fever of my brain; to think no more of my situation, so sad, so undeserved.

Forgive me, my darling, if sometimes I complain. What would you, at times memory is so bitter! I need to throw myself upon your breast, there to pour out my overburdened heart. We have always understood each other's thoughts so well, my darling, that I am sure that your strong and generous heart beats with the indignation of my own.

We were so happy—everything in life smiled upon us. Do you remember when I told you that we had nothing for which to envy any one; that all was ours? Position, fortune, the love we bore each other, our adorable little children—we had everything.

There was not a cloud on the horizon; then came the

awful thunderbolt, so unexpected, so unbelievable! Even now it seems sometimes that I must be the victim of a horrible nightmare.

I do not complain of physical sufferings, you know that I despise them; but to know that an accusation of infamy stains my name, when I am innocent—oh, no! no! This is why I have borne all my torment, all the anguish, all the insults. I am convinced that soon or late the truth will come to light, and then they will do me justice.

I can easily excuse this anger, this rage of all the people—the noble people, who have been taught to believe that there is a traitor; but I want to live so that they may know that the traitor is not I.

Upheld by your love, by the boundless love of all of ours, I shall overcome fatality. I do not say that I shall not still have moments of despondency, even of despair. Truly not to complain of an error so monstrous would require a grandeur of soul to which I cannot pretend. But my heart will remain strong and valiant.

Then courage and energy, my darling. We must all be brave and strong. Let us lift up our heads all of us, carry them high and proudly. We are martyrs. I will live, my adored one, because I will that you shall bear my name, as you have borne it until now, with honor, with joy, and with love; and because I will to transmit it to our children without a stain.

Therefore do not allow yourselves to be beaten down by adversity—neither you nor the others. Search for the truth without parleying, without a truce.

As to me, I shall wait with the strength born of a pure and tranquil conscience until this mysterious and tragical affair is dragged into the light.

You know, moreover, my darling, that the only mercy I have ever asked for is the truth; I hope that my countrymen will not fail in the duty which they owe to a fellow-man, who asks one right only—that the search for the truth may be kept up.

And when the light shines in on my vindication; when they give me back my *galons* that I won, and that I am as worthy to wear now as when I won them by my own might; when I am once more in my own place, at the head of my troopers, oh, then, my darling, I shall forget everything—the sufferings, the torture, the insults, the bleeding wounds.

May God and human justice grant that the day break soon!

Until to-morrow, my adored Lucie! Then shall I have the pleasure of embracing you again. Now I am counting the hours; to-morrow I shall count the minutes.

I embrace you fondly.

ALFRED.

Good, long kisses to our two darlings. I dare not think of them. Talk to them about me. Let not these young souls suffer from our sadness. Embrace every one at home for me.

---

12 January, 1895, Saturday, 4 o'clock.

How short was that half hour yesterday! I arrange in my mind in advance just how I shall employ every minute, so that I may not forget what I want to say. Then the time goes by as in a dream; and all at once the interview is over, and again I have said almost nothing.

LETTERS OF AN INNOCENT MAN

How can two beings like you and me be so cruelly tried?

Do you remember the charming plans that we had sketched out for this very winter? We ought to profit a little by our liberty when we are together to go back to those days when, two young lovers, we wandered together in the land of the sun. Ah, it cannot be possible! All this anguish, all that is passing now, is inhuman. If there is a God, if there is any justice in this world, we must believe that the truth must declare itself soon; that we shall be recompensed for all that we have suffered.

I have put the children's photographs before me on the little table of my cell. When I look at them the tears rush to my eyes, my heart bursts—but at the same time it does me good, it strengthens my courage. Bring me your photograph, too. Your three faces before my eyes will be the companions of my mournful solitude.

Ah, my darling wife, you have a noble mission to fulfil, and for it you need all your energy. That is why I am always begging of you to care for your health. Your physical strength is more necessary than ever before. You owe yourself to your children first, then to the name they bear. It must be proven to the whole world that that name is pure and stainless.

Oh, for light upon my tragic situation! How I long for it! How I wait for it! How I would buy it if I could, not only with all my fortune—that would be nothing—but with my very blood!

If only I could put my brain to sleep! If I could prevent it from thinking always of this unexplainable mystery! I long to pierce the shadows; I long to tear up the earth that the daylight may burst through.

You will answer, and with justice, that I must be patient; that time is necessary to discover the truth. Alas! I know it. But what would you? The minutes to me seem hours. It always seems to me that some one will come to me in another minute and say:

"Forgive us, we were deceived; the mistake has been discovered."

Now I am waiting for Monday. Henceforth the weeks for me are composed but of the two days when you come to visit me. You cannot know how I marvel at your self-sacrifice, your heroism, how I draw courage from your love, so profound, so devoted.

Thank your sister Alice for her excellent letter, which has given me great pleasure. Give news of me to all the members of the family to whom I cannot write. Tell them that their letters are always most welcome.

I embrace you tenderly, fondly.

ALFRED.

---

14 January, 1895, Monday, 9 o'clock in the morning.

At last the happy day has come again when I can have the happiness of seeing you, of kissing you, of receiving news by word of mouth of you all. I have so many things to tell you; but when I see you shall not I again, in the emotion which will seize me, forget everything? Last night again I could not sleep until two o'clock. I was thinking of you, of you all, of this fearful enigma which I long to decipher. I have turned over in my mind a thousand ways, each more violent, more extravagant than the other, by which to rend the veil which shields the monster.

How can I help it, my darling? Night and day I

think only of that. My mind is always straining to reach that end, and I cannot help you in any way. It is the feeling of my utter helplessness which hurts me most.

I try hard to read, but while my eyes follow the lines my thoughts wander.

And now, immediately, my darling, I am to have the joy of seeing you!

Waiting for that moment, I pace my cell like a lion in its cage.

---

14 January, 1895, 1 o'clock.

The time drags slowly; the minutes are hours. How can I use up my energy! How can I restrain my heart! Sometimes I lose my patience. It is not the courage, the energy that I lack—you know it well—and my conscience gives me superhuman force, but it is this terrible idleness, this longing to be able to help you to pursue the only object of my life, to discover the wretch who has stolen my honor; this is what burns in my blood. Ah, I would rather mount alone to the assault of ten redoubts than be here powerless, inactive, waiting passively for the truth to be revealed! I envy the man who breaks stones on the highway, absorbed in his mechanical labor. But, my darling, I shall soon see you now, and you will give me back my patience.

---

3 o'clock.

Already the time has passed as in a dream, . . . and I had so many things to tell you, . . . and then when I am

CAPTAIN ALFRED DREYFUS

This portrait is enlarged from a photograph taken on the occasion of his degradation

in your presence I look at you, I no longer can remember anything. All that happens to me then appears a dream; it seems to me that never again shall we be separated—that I am awaking from my horrible nightmare. But alas! then comes reality—our parting.

Ah, the wretch who committed the crime—who stole our honor! It is no ordinary punishment that he deserves. When the day comes and his guilt is known I hope that public opinion may nail his name to the pillory of history, that his punishment may be beyond all that we can imagine.

I ask you to forgive me for my weakness, for my impatience. But think, my darling, what these long hours are to me—these long days.

But I am calmer after each interview. I draw new strength, a new store of patience from your looks, from your love.

Ah, the truth! We must reveal it, it must shine forth clear and luminous. I live only for that; I live only by that hope.

And this truth, as you have so truly said, must be entire, absolute—there must be left no doubt in the mind of any one. My innocence must burst forth. Everybody—all must recognize it—they must know that my honor stands as high as that of any man on the earth.

And it is to this end that I must be patient. . . . I realize it as you do, . . . but the heart has reasons that reason knows not! If I could only put my brain to sleep until the day when they find the guilty one I should bear physical torments valiantly, I should not waver. And then think of the atmosphere that is to envelop me on the path I have yet to follow!

But my heart must be silent. I gain each time new strength, new patience, from your dear eyes.

Do not think any longer of my sufferings. You can comfort me only in doing as you have done—in searching for the guilty one, without a thought of truce—without an hour of rest.

I have read Pierrot's few lines in Marie's letter. Thank them both, particularly the hand that directed the hand of Pierrot.

Make of our dear children vigorous and healthy beings.

I embrace you as I love you.

ALFRED.

Tuesday, 15 January, 1895, 9 o'clock in the morning.
My Darling:

I was thinking a great deal last night of what you said yesterday when you urged me to be patient; when you explained to me that nothing is done in a day. Alas! I know it well; but I suffer precisely because of my good qualities, which are defects situated as we are now. I am an active man, and I am impatient to have it deciphered—this enigma that is torturing my brain.

But you understand, my darling, since you know me so well. It is useless for me to tell each day of the fevers of impatience which at times overcome me; the paroxysms of crazy anger which at times carry me away....

Yesterday I received good news. They told me that I am to see your mother to-day. I am rejoicing over it in advance.

LETTERS OF AN INNOCENT MAN

Half-past 5 o'clock.

I have seen Me. Demange for a few minutes; afterward I had the pleasure of seeing your mother.

I was so enervated to-day that I almost fainted before her. I could not help it. Sometimes I become again a man, with all man's weakness, with all man's passions. You must admit that there is in my situation enough to break down the strongest.

Ah, believe that were it not for you—for our dear children—it would be far easier for me to die! But I must bear up and face my sorrow. I must tell myself that I will bear all the agony, all the martyrdom, until the time when my innocence shall burst forth in the light of day.

It is impossible that it can be otherwise.

I shall hold out to the end, be sure of it; but at times I will give way to cries of wrath—to cries of anguish.

Embrace them all, our darlings, for me.

    Your devoted
        ALFRED.

---

7 o'clock.

My moment of weakness is past. I see and I live in the future. Courage, then, all of us. Sooner or later innocence will triumph.

Go forward without flinching on the path you have marked out, as I shall go forward without weakening on my dolorous journey.

LETTERS OF AN INNOCENT MAN

Wednesday, 16 January, 1895,
10 o'clock in the morning.

My Darling:

I have succeeded in conquering my nerves. I have silenced the tumult of my soul. It does no good to be impatient, since I am resolved to live to see my innocence proclaimed.

I know that it will require time—yes, a long time—but I shall wait, as I promised you that I would, with calmness and with dignity until the truth is known. My conscience will give me the necessary strength.

I will prepare my soul to bear without a murmur the suffering which yet awaits me. I will stifle the sobs of my bleeding heart.

Yesterday I lost for some minutes the sense of my existence; remember that it is now three months that I have been shut up in this room, a prey to the most appalling mental tortures that can be inflicted upon a man of heart; but by a violent effort of my whole being I regained possession of myself.

It is, above all, my nerves that are weak; my spirit is what it was in the beginning.

But you all are united in will, in intelligence, and in devotion; therefore I have the conviction that soon or late the day will dawn. I shall not belie your efforts.

Let us speak no more of it.

What shall I tell you? My daily life? You know it! I have described it to you in its smallest details. My thoughts? They are all of you, of our dear children, of our dear families. Still two more days to wait before I can see you and embrace you. How long the interval is that separates our interviews, and how short the time of our meetings! I would make the time run by when you are far from me. I would make it an eternity when you are with me.

What courage you give me to live, my darling; what patience I draw from the deep well of your eyes, from the memories you recall to me, from my duty to our darlings.

1 o'clock.

I have just received your two dear letters of Tuesday. You are right to speak to me of our dear ones. Though every thought of them rends my heart, their chatter, which you repeat to me, awakes in me happy and touching memories, and faith comes back to me—a faith in better days.

I agree absolutely with you as to the work in which you are engaged. Calmness, time, and perseverance are needful if we would go on to the end. I know it well; I should do just as you are doing were I in your place, preferring to advance slowly but surely rather than lose all by thoughtless haste. But I, alas! I am shut up between four walls, idle, my blood on fire and my point of view is necessarily different from yours.

They have just told me that my two sisters will come to see me at two o'clock. What a happiness it is to see those who belong to one!

5 o'clock.

I have seen Louise and Rachel. I have felt that their hearts beat with mine, that they share my sufferings. Their faith in the future is absolute. I hope as they do.

What devotion I meet in our wonderful families, in our friends! It consoles me, moreover, for the weakness of humanity. Truly we can judge of people only when we are in trouble.

I embrace you a thousand times, as I love you.

Your devoted
ALFRED.

Dear Jeanne must be changing in her appearance. Is she becoming as handsome as a girl as her brother is handsome as a boy?

Thursday, 17 January, 1895, 9 o'clock.

What a part these accursed nerves play in human life! Why cannot we entirely disengage our material being from our moral personality, so that one shall not influence the other?

My moral personality is always salient, always strong, as ever resolved to go on to the end; it is determined to face all. I must get back my honor that they tore from me, although I had never faltered. But my material personality is subjected to rude shocks. My nerves, which have been too tensely strung during nearly three months, make me suffer horribly at times, and I have not even the resource of violent physical exercise by which to subdue them. I am to be given some medicine to-day to relax their tension.

Ah, when I think of those who have accused me and caused my condemnation! May remorse pursue them and make them bear the anguish that I am bearing. But let us talk of other things.

How are you, my darling? How are the children? I hope that you all may continue to be well. Be careful of yourself; you have not the right to allow yourself to be broken down. You have need of all your courage and of all your energy; and therefore you need all your physical strength.

At last the time has come. To-morrow will be Friday. How long that day is in coming! Happily the time seemed a little less long this week; for yesterday and the day before I heard of you from those who came to see me.

After all, why should not I, too, have confidence, when I feel around me all this friendship, all this affection, all this devotion!

But that which I must have above all things is patience.

2 o'clock.

They have given me your letter of yesterday. I find that I moan enough of my own accord without encouragement from you to do so still more. Ah, how terrible this helplessness is, when I long to cry aloud my innocence, proclaim it, prove it! Well, all this will do no good. It is necessary, as I cannot reiterate too often, as every one must have told you for me—it is necessary to search on without truce, without rest.

The will is a lever which pries up and breaks in pieces all obstacles.

Yesterday I received a good letter from your sister; to-day one from your mother. I have, alas! nothing in particular to tell them. My life, you know it hour by hour. You can describe it to them as completely as I could. Tell your mother that she must not fear anything. I have nervous weakness, which is easily explained, but my mind remains strong. My soul needs the truth, it demands its honor, and it shall have it. I shall not belie your efforts.

Sooner or later, my darling, our happiness will return to us. I have the firm conviction of this. The hardest of all is to have the patience that is absolutely necessary. Happy is it for you that you have a powerful diversion—action.

Until to-morrow, my darling, when I shall have the pleasure of seeing you, of talking with you, of kissing you!

A thousand kisses.

Your devoted husband,
ALFRED.

Good kisses to the dear ones.

JANUARY AND FEBRUARY, 1895.
THE PRISON OF SAINT-MARTIN DE RE.

19 January, 1895.

My Darling:

Thursday evening, toward ten o'clock, they came to wake me to bring me here, where I arrived only last night. I do not want to speak of my journey, it would break your heart. Know only that I have heard the legitimate cries of a brave and generous people against him whom they believe to be a traitor, the lowest of wretches. I am no longer sure if I have a heart.

Oh, what a sacrifice I made the day of my condemnation, when I promised you that I should not kill myself! What a sacrifice I made to the name of my poor, dear, little children, in bearing what I am undergoing! If there is a divine justice, we must hope that I shall be recompensed for this long and fearful torture, for this suffering of every minute and every instant. The other day your father told me that he would have preferred death. And I—I would rather, a hundred thousand times rather, be dead. But this right to die belongs to none of us; the more I suffer the more must it impel your courage and your resolution to find the truth. Look on for the truth, do not waver, do not rest. Let your efforts be in proportion to the sufferings which I have imposed upon myself.

Will you please ask, or have some one ask, at the Ministry for the following authorizations; the Minister alone can accord them:

1. The right to write to all the members of my family—father, mother, brothers, and sisters.

2. The right to write and to work in my cell. At present I have neither *paper,* nor *pen,* nor *ink.* I am given only the sheet of paper on which I write to you; then they take away my pen and ink.

3. Permission to smoke.

I beg you not to come before you are completely cured.

The climate here is very rigorous, and you need all your health, first for our dear children, then for the end for which you are working. *As to my régime here, I am forbidden to speak to you of it.*

And now I must remind you that before you come here you must provide yourself with *all* the authorizations necessary *to see me;* do not forget to ask permission *to kiss me,* etc., etc.

When shall we be reunited, my darling? I live in the hope of that, and in the still greater hope of my restoration to honor. But oh, how my soul suffers! Tell all our family that they must work on without weakening, without resting; for all that comes to us now is appalling, tragic. Write to me soon.

I embrace you as I love you.

ALFRED.

Tuesday, 21 January, 1895, 9 o'clock in the morning.

How you must suffer! . . . The tragedy of which we are the victims is certainly the most terrible of the century. To have everything—happiness, the future, a charming home—and then, all at once, to be accused and condemned for a crime so monstrous!

Ah, the monster who has cast dishonor in our family might better have killed me; at least there would then have been only me to suffer! This is what tortures me the most; it is the thought of the infamy that is coupled with my name. If I had only physical sufferings to bear, it would be nothing. Sufferings borne for a noble cause are elevating; but to suffer because I am condemned for an infamous crime—ah, no! Cannot you see that it is too much, even for energy like mine?

Oh, why am I not dead? I have not even the right to leave this life of my own will; it would be an act of cowardice. I have not the right to die, to look for oblivion, until I shall have regained my honor. The other day when they insulted me at La Rochelle, I wished that I might escape from the hands of my guards and present myself with naked breast to those to whom I was a just object of indignation and say to them: "Do not insult me; my heart that you cannot know is pure and free from all defilement; but if you believe me guilty, here, take my body; I give it up to you without regret."

At least then, when under the sharp sting of physical suffering, I should still have cried, "*Vive la France!*" Perhaps then they would have believed in my innocence.

After all, what do I beg for night and day? Justice, justice! Are we in the nineteenth century, or must we turn back for centuries? Is it possible that innocence can be unrecognized in a century of light and truth? They must search for the truth. I do not ask for mercy, but I demand the justice due to every human creature. They must search. Let those who possess powerful means of investigation use them to this end; it is a sacred duty which they owe to humanity and justice. It is impossible that light shall not be thrown upon my mysterious and tragic fate.

O God! who will give me back my honor that has been stolen from me, basely stolen from me? Oh, what a dark drama, my poor darling! As you have so truly said, it surpasses anything that can be imagined.

I have but two happy moments in my days, but so short. The first is when they bring me this sheet of paper so that I can write to you—I pass a few moments in talking with you. The second is when they bring me your daily letter. The rest of the time I am alone with my thoughts; and God knows that they are sad and dark.

When is this horrible drama to end? When will the truth at last be known? Oh, my fortune, all of it, to the one who is adroit, able enough, to solve this sad enigma!

Tell me about all our friends.

Embrace them all for me.

I dare not speak of our darlings. When I look at their photographs, when I see their eyes so good, so sweet, the sobs rise from my heart to my lips. When we suffer for some thing or for some one it is easy to understand. . . . But why and, above all, for whom am I suffering this odious martyrdom?

I press you to my heart.

ALFRED.

Do not come until you are completely recovered and in excellent health. Our children have need of you.

---

23 January, 1895.

My Darling:

I receive your letters every day. As yet they have given me none from any member of the family, and, on my side, I have not yet received the authorization to write to them. I have written to you every day since Saturday. I hope that you have received all my letters.

You must not be astonished, my darling, at the scene of La Rochelle. I find it perfectly natural. What astonishes me is that no one has yet been found to come forward and tell what our families really are—families whose names are synonymous with loyalty and honor. Ah, human cowardice, I have measured its length and breadth in these sad, dark days!

When I think of what I was but a few months ago, and when I compare it with my miserable situation today, I confess that my heart faints, that I give way to ferocious outbreaks against the injustice of my lot. Truly I am the victim of the most hideous error of our century. At times my reason refuses to believe it; it seems to me that I am the dupe of a terrible hallucination, that it will all vanish; . . . but, alas! the reality is all around me.

Why did not we all die before the beginning of this tragedy? Truly it would have been preferable. And now we have not the right to die, not one of us has that right. We must live to cleanse our name of the stain with which it has been sullied. My conviction is absolute; I am sure that sooner or later the light will shine out. It is impossible in an age like ours that search shall not result in the discovery of the one who is really guilty; but what shall I be, mentally and physically, at that time? I believe that life will have no more attraction for me, and if I cling to it, it will be for your sake, my dear heart, whose devotion has been heroic through all these terrible hours—for you and for my dear children, to whom I wish to restore their honorable name.

But whatever may come, I am sure that history will place things in their true position. There will be in our dear country of France, so easily excited, but so generous to innocent sufferers, some man honest and courageous enough to try to find the truth.

And I, my darling, what can I say to you? That my heart is broken; at least they will have accomplished that. But be tranquil; until my last breath I shall stand firm. I will not weaken, nor bow my head.

My honor is equal to that of any man on the earth. I demand justice; you also must demand it. This is all the mercy that I beg for. I ask for nothing but the truth—the whole truth.

And this truth, if we pursue it steadfastly, we shall have at last; it is impossible that such an error can rest unexposed.

LETTERS OF AN INNOCENT MAN

When I look back, my sufferings are so appalling that I am seized by terrible nervous shocks. I look forward always with the hope that soon all will be made clear and that they will give me back my honor—the thing I hold dearest in this world.

May God and justice grant that it may be soon! Truly I have suffered enough. We all have suffered enough.

I hope that you always take good care of your health. You need, my darling, all your physical strength to be able to bear the moral tortures that are inflicted upon you.

How are all the members of our two families? Give me news of them, since I cannot hear directly from them.

Kiss our two darlings for me—my love to all the family.

I embrace you with all my strength.

ALFRED.

---

24 January, 1895.

My dear Lucie:

I see by your letter dated Tuesday, that as yet you have not heard from me. How you must suffer, my poor darling! What horrible martyrdom for us both! Are we unfortunate enough? Oh, what have we done that we must bear such misfortune! It is this that makes it so appalling that we must ask ourselves of what crime we have been culpable, what sin we are expiating.

Ah, the monster who has cast shame and dishonor into the midst of an honorable family! Such a one deserves absolutely no mercy. His crime is so terrible that reason refuses to comprehend such infamy joined to such cowardice. To me it seems impossible that such machinations shall not soon or late be discovered, that such a crime can rest unpunished.

Last night there was a moment when the reality of my position seemed to me a dream, horrible, strange, supernatural, from which I tried to arouse myself, to awake. But, alas! it was not a dream. I tried to escape from this awful nightmare, to find myself again in my own real life, such as it ought to be, among you all, in your arms, my darling, with my dear children by our side.

Ah, when shall this blessed day arrive? To that end spare neither time nor effort nor money. Even if I am ruined as far as my fortune goes, I do not care for that; but I want my honor; it is for that that I bear these cruel tortures. Alas! I bear them as best I can. There are times when I have moments of crushing despondency; when it seems to me that death would be a thousand times preferable to the torture of soul that I endure; but by a violent effort of the will I regain possession of myself. What would you? I must at times give my grief free course; I can bear it with more firmness afterward.

After all, let us hope that this horrible agony may end—that is my only reason for living, that is my only hope.

The days and the nights are long. My brain is always searching for the answer to this appalling riddle that it cannot solve.

Oh, if only I might, with the sharp blade of my sword, tear aside the impenetrable veil that surrounds my tragic fate! It is impossible that in the end this shall not be done.

LETTERS OF AN INNOCENT MAN

Tell me everything that concerns you all, because yours are the only letters I receive. Tell me of our dear children, of your own health.

I embrace you as I love you.

ALFRED.

Friday, 25 January, 1895.

My dear Lucie:

Your letter of yesterday wrung my heart. The sorrow transpierced every word.

Never, surely, have two unfortunate creatures suffered as we suffer. If I had not faith in the future, if my conscience, clean and pure, did not tell me that such an error cannot exist eternally, I should, of a truth, give way to the darkest thoughts. I should despair. Once, as you know, I determined to kill myself; I yielded to your remonstrances; I have promised you to live, for you have made me realize that I have not the right to desert my post; because I am innocent I must live. But alas! if you could know how, sometimes, it is more difficult to live than to die!

But be tranquil, my darling; no matter how I am tortured I shall not belie your generous efforts. I will live . . . as long as my physical strength and, above all, my moral strength hold out.

All night long I thought of you, my darling; I suffered with you. I have written to you every day since last Saturday. I hope that by this time you have received all my letters.

I do not know either on whom or on what to fix my ideas. When I look back to the past anger rises to my brain, so impossible it seems to me that everything has been thus wrested from me. When I look to the present, my plight is so wretched that my thoughts turn toward death, in which I might forget all my misery. It is only when I look forward to the future that I have a moment of consolation, for, as I have just told you, hope is all that gives me life.

Just now I gazed for several minutes at the pictures of our dear children; but I could not bear to look at them longer; my sobs strangled me. Yes, my darling, I must live. I must bear my martyrdom to the end, for the name borne by these dear little ones. Some day they must learn that this name is worthy to be honored, to be respected; they must be sure that if I hold the honor of many men below my own, there is none that I hold above it.

Ah, surely it is full time that this horrible suffering to which we are all subjected should end! I dare not think of it. Everything within me swells my heart to bursting.

I embrace you a thousand, thousand times, and our good darlings.

ALFRED.

Friday, 4 o'clock.

They have given me your letter of Friday, in which you tell me that you have received my last letter. You are asked to abstain from making any reflections upon the measures taken in regard to us. Henceforth I shall no longer have the right to write to you more than twice a week. You can write to me every day. Do it, my darling, for that is the only thing that gives me courage to live. If I could not feel your warm affection, the love of all of ours, struggling with me for my honor, I should not have the courage to pursue this almost superhuman task. They still give me no letters from any of the family, and I am not permitted to write to them. The Minister is the only one who can modify this state of things.

You cannot imagine, my poor child, how unhappy I am. Night and day I think of the horrible word that is coupled with my name; there are times when my brain refuses to admit such a thing. I ask myself, in my agitated nights, if I am awake or if I sleep. Added to everything else I have no occupation by which to distract my sombre thoughts.

I kiss you a thousand times, and also all the others.

ALFRED.

28 January, 1895.

My dear Lucie:

This is one of the happy days of my sad existence, because I can come to pass half an hour with you, talking to you and telling you of my life. You know that I am permitted to write to you but twice a week. I have received your two letters, of Friday and Saturday. Each time that they bring me a letter from you a ray of joy pierces to my wounded heart. What you told me in your letter of Saturday is perfectly true. Like you, I have the absolute conviction that all will be discovered, but when? You know that in the end everything is blunted, even the most heroic courage. And, then, between the courage that makes a man confront danger—no matter what danger it may be—and the courage that enables him to bear, without fainting, the worst of outrages, scorn and shame, there is a great difference. I have never lowered my head, believe it; my conscience forbade that. I have a right to look all the world in the face. But, alas! all the world cannot look into my soul, into my conscience. The fact is there, brutal and terrible. That is why each time that I receive one of your dear letters I have a ray of hope; I hope at last to hear some good news. If the Léons have come back to Paris, their impatience not letting them wait, only think how it is with me. I know that you all suffer as I do, that you partake of my anguish and my tortures, but you have your activity to distract you, a little, from this awful sorrow; while I am here, impatient, shut up alone night and day with my thoughts.

I ask myself even now how my brain has been strong enough to resist so many and so oft-repeated blows; how is it that I have not gone mad.

It is certain, my darling, that it is only your profound love which can make me still hold on to life. To have consecrated all my strength, all my intelligence, to the service of my country, and then suddenly to be accused of the greatest, the most monstrous, crime a soldier can commit—condemned for it—that is enough to disgust one with life! When my honor is given back to me—oh, may that day come soon!—then I will consecrate myself entirely to you and to our dear children.

And then think of the terrible way I have still to traverse before I shall arrive at the end of my journey—crossing the seas for sixty or eighty days under conditions so appalling. I do not speak—you know it—of the material conditions of the passage; you know that my body has never worried me much; but the moral conditions! To be during all that time before sailors, the officers of the navy—that is, before honest and loyal soldiers—who will see in me a traitor, the most abject of criminals! At the bare thought of it my heart shrinks.

I think that no innocent man in this world has ever endured the mental torments that I have already borne, that I have still to bear. So you can think that in each of your letters I search for that word of hope, so long waited for, so ardently desired.

Write to me, each day, long letters. Give me news of all the members of the family, since I do not hear from them and cannot write to them. Your letters give me, as I have already said, my only moments of happiness. You only, you alone, bind me to life.

Look backward I cannot. The tears blind me when I think of our lost happiness. I can look forward only in the supreme hope that soon the day will break, illumined with the light of truth.

Kiss them all for me; kiss our dear children. A thousand kisses for you. ALFRED.

Thursday, 31 January, 1895.

My dear Lucie:

At last the happy day is here! I can write to you. I count them, alas! my happy days.

I have not, indeed, received any letters from you since the one they gave me last Sunday. What terrible suffering! Until now I have had each day a moment of happiness in receiving your letter. It was an echo from you all—an echo of the sympathy of you all, that warmed my poor frozen heart. I used to read and reread your letters. I absorbed each word. Little by little the written words were transformed and given a voice—it seemed to me that I could hear you speaking; that you were by my side. Oh, the delicious music that whispered to my soul! Now, for four days nothing but my dreary sorrow, the appalling solitude.

Truly I ask myself how I live. Night and day my sole companion is my brain. I have nothing to do except to weep over our misfortunes.

Last night when I thought of all my past life, of all my labor, of all that I have done in order to acquire an honorable position, . . . then when I compared that with my present lot, sobs seized my throat; it seemed that my heart was being torn asunder; and, so that my guards should not hear me—I was so ashamed of my weakness—I stifled my sobs with the coverings of my bed.

Oh, it is too cruel!

How I prove to-day by my own experience that it is sometimes harder to live than to die!

To die would be to pass a moment of suffering; but it would be to forget all my woes, all my tortures.

On the other hand, to carry each day the weight of suffering, to feel the heart bleed, and to endure this torment in every nerve, to feel every fibre of my being tremble, to suffer the undying martyrdom of the heart, this is terrible.

But I have not the right to die. We have none of us that right. We shall have it only after the truth shall have been brought to light; only when my honor shall have been given back to me. Until then we must live. I bend every effort to this task, to live. I try to annihilate in me all my intellectual part, all that is sensible of suffering, so that I may live, like a beast, preoccupied with the satisfying of its material needs.

When shall this martyrdom come to an end? When will men recognize the truth?

How are our poor darlings? When I think of them it is a torrent of tears. And you, I hope that you are well. You must take care of your health, my darling. The children first of all, and then the mission which you have to fulfill, impose upon you duties which you cannot neglect.

Forgive the disconnected and wandering style of my writing. I no longer know how to write; the words will not come to me, my brain is shattered. There is but one fixed idea in my mind—the hope of some day knowing the truth, of seeing my innocence recognized and proclaimed. That is what I mutter night and day, in my dreams as in my waking hours.

When shall I be able to embrace you and recover in your deep love the strength I need to carry me to the end of my calvary?

Embrace every one for me.

Kisses for the darlings.

I embrace you as I love you.

ALFRED.

Sunday, 3 February, 1895.

My Darling:

I have passed an atrocious week. I have been without a word from you since last Sunday—that is to say, for eight days. I thought that you must be sick, then that one of the children was sick, then, in my reeling brain, I conjured up all kinds of suppositions—I imagined everything.

You can realize, my darling, all that I have suffered, all that I still suffer. In my horrible solitude, in the tragic situation in which events as unnatural as they are incomprehensible have placed me, I had at least one consolation; it was to feel that you were near me, your heart beating in unison with mine and sharing all my tortures.

The night between Thursday and Friday, above all, was appalling. I will not tell you about it; it would rend your heart. All that I can tell you is that my mind kept going over and over the accusation they had brought against me. I told myself that the thing was impossible. . . . Then I aroused myself, and I realized the sad truth of it all.

Oh, why cannot they open my heart and read there as one reads in an open book; there, at least, they would see the sentiments which I have always professed and which I still hold. No, no, it seems to me impossible that all this is to endure eternally. Some day the truth must come to light. By an unheard-of effort of the will I regained my self-control; I told myself that I could neither go down into my grave nor go mad with a dishonored name. I must live then, whatever may be the torture of soul to which I am a prey.

Oh, this opprobrium, this infamy covering my name! When will they be taken away?

May it come, the blessed day when my innocence is recognized! when they give me back that honor that never failed me! I am tired of suffering.

Let them take my blood, let them do what they will

with my body, . . . you know that I do not care a straw for that; . . . but let them give me back my honor.

Will no one hear this cry of despair, this cry of an innocent wretch who begs only for justice—only justice?

Each day I hope that the hour is at hand, that men are now to recognize what I have been, what I am—a loyal soldier, worthy to lead the soldiers of France under fire. Then the night comes, and nothing, still nothing.

Add to this that I received no letter from you; that I am absolutely alone with my torture of soul, and you can judge of my condition. But be reassured, I am strong again. I have called myself a coward; I have told myself all that you yourself could have told me were you at my side; an innocent man has never the right to despair. Then, though I have no news of you, I feel that all your hearts, all your souls, are throbbing in unison with my heart and with my soul; that you suffer with me the infamy that covers my name and that you are endeavoring to wipe it out. When can you come to pass some hours with me? How happy I should be could I but draw new strength from your heart!

Shall I have a letter from you to-day? I dare not hope too much, since each day my hope is deferred, and at each disappointment the suffering is too great.

Well, my darling, what can I tell you? I live by hope. Night and day I see before me, like a brilliant star, the moment when all shall be forgotten, when my honor shall be given back to me.

Kiss my darlings tenderly, most tenderly, for me.

I send kisses for all the members of our families.

As for you, I embrace you, as I love you, with all my strength. ALFRED.

LETTERS OF AN INNOCENT MAN

Thursday, 7 February, 1895.

My good Lucie:

On Sunday I received a package of fifteen letters all dated before Sunday, January 27. Thank all the members of the family for their warm affection, which I have never doubted. I am still without news of you for more than ten days. To tell you my tortures is impossible.

To find myself thus confronted by soldiers whom yesterday I was so proud to command, whom I am as worthy to command to-day, and who see in me the lowest of wretches—oh, it is appalling! At the very thought my heart stops its beating.

My story is too horrible, my brain can bear no more.

I have been able to resist thus far because my heart, honest and pure, told me that it was my duty; that my innocence, so complete and so absolute, must soon be made manifest; but this long-continued outrage is heart-breaking.

I would rather have stood before the execution squad; at least then there could have been no possible discussion, and you could afterward have rehabilitated my memory.

But do not fear that I shall ever attempt to take my life. I have promised you never to do it, and you know that I have but one word. Therefore do not be anxious in regard to that. But how far will my strength carry me, how long will my heart continue to beat in this atmosphere of scorn, I, so proud of my stainless honor, I, so haughty, that is what I cannot tell!

Ah, if there were nothing worse than bodily torture to be borne, if it were only that I must suffer, waiting for the truth, I should be strong enough to bear this appalling martyrdom. But to bear scorn, . . . and for so long, . . . it is horrible!

I do not believe that there has ever been an innocent man who has endured tortures to be compared to mine.

As for you, my poor and well-beloved wife, you must keep all your courage and all your energy. It is in the name of our profound love that I beg you to do this, for you must be there to wash away from my name the stain with which it has been sullied. You must be there to bring up our children to be brave and honorable. You must be there to tell them, one day, what their father was—a brave and loyal soldier, crushed by an appalling fatality.

Shall I have news of you to-day? When shall I be told that I may have the pleasure and the joy of embracing you? Each day I hope it, and nothing comes to lighten the burden of my horrible agony.

Courage, my darling, you need so much of it—so much! You all need it, all of our two families. You have not the right to let yourself break down, for you have a great mission to fulfill, no matter what may become of me. Give them all my love; embrace our two poor darlings tenderly for me, and receive for yourself the tenderest kisses of him who loves you so dearly.

ALFRED.

Sunday, 10 February, 1895.

My dear Lucie:

I received, Friday evening, your letters up to and including that of the 2d of February. I saw with pleasure that you are all well. I hope that you have received my letters. I shall not speak to you of myself; you must understand the slow agony of my heart. But it will serve no purpose to complain. What you need, what you must all have, is steadfast courage. You must not allow yourself to be beaten down by adversity, however terrible it may be.

You must succeed in proving throughout the length and breadth of France that I was a worthy and a loyal soldier, who loved his country above everything, who served it with devotion always.

That is the principal, the essential object, far above my own being, my personal fate. There is a name that must be washed free from the stain with which it has been sullied, a name, until now pure and spotless, that must shine again as pure as in former days. It is the name that our dear children bear, and that in itself should give you all the necessary courage.

I thank you for all the news you give me of our friends. I, too, regret that I cannot write to them. You know how dearly I love them all. Kiss my relations tenderly for me, your dear family and mine. Tell them what I think, what I would convince you of; it is that I personally am only the secondary consideration, that there is a name to be cleansed from dishonor.

No one must falter until this supreme task has been accomplished. To speak to you of the condition I am in is useless. As I said above, your heart tells you far better than my pen could tell. I will go on as long as my heart still beats, having before me night and day the supreme hope that the place that I deserve will be restored to me.

You see, darling, a man of honor cannot live without his honor. It does no good to tell himself that he is innocent; it is an unceasing gnawing of the heart. In solitude the hours are long, and my mind cannot comprehend all that has come upon me. Never could a romancer, however rich his imagination, have written a story more tragic.

I am convinced, as you are, that sooner or later the truth will come to light. The just cause always triumphs; but when that day comes what shall my condition be? It is that that I cannot tell. . . . There is always my aching heart, which from morning till night, and from night till morning, beats as if to burst.

I hope that they will let me kiss you at least before I set out upon my journey.

I thank you for all you tell me about the children. You must bring them up seriously and give them a thorough education; be as careful of their bodies as you are of their minds and hearts. I know what you are; I have no uneasiness on this score. Indeed, I know that you will bring them up to be generous and noble souls, eager for all that is good and beautiful, marching forward always in the way of duty.

Kiss the good darlings for me a thousand, thousand times.

I pray you give every one my love. Receive the most ardent kisses of your husband, who loves you, who lives only in the thought of you.

ALFRED.

14 February, 1895.

My dear Lucie:

The few minutes that I passed with you were very sweet to me, although it was impossible for me to tell you all that I had within my heart.

LETTERS OF AN INNOCENT MAN

My time passed while I looked at you, trying to impress your image upon my very being, asking myself by what inconceivable fatality I was separated from you.

Some day when they will tell my story it will seem unbelievable. But what we must tell ourselves now is that I must be rehabilitated. My name must shine anew with all the lustre it should never have lost. I would rather see my children dead than think that the name which they bear is a dishonored one.

This is a vital question for us all. It is not possible to live without honor. I cannot tell you this often enough.

I shall soon come to a new station on my dolorous way.

I do not fear bodily suffering; but oh, my God, that I might be spared the torture of my soul! I am tired of feeling that my name is scorned—I, so proud, so uplifted, just because my name was above reproach; I, who had the right to look the whole world in the face. I live only in the hope of seeing my name soon cleansed from this horrible stain. You have again given me back my courage. Your noble abnegation, your heroic devotion, give me renewed strength to bear my terrible martyrdom.

I shall not tell you that I love you yet more; you know how profound my love is for you. It is that love that enables me to bear my tortures of mind. It is the love of all of you for me.

Embrace them all tenderly for me, the members of our two families, your dear parents, our children, and, for yourself, receive the best, the tenderest kisses of your devoted husband.

ALFRED.

LETTERS OF AN INNOCENT MAN

21 February, 1895.

My dear Lucie:

When I see you the time is so short, I am so distracted at seeing the hour slipping away with a rapidity that I cannot realize—the hours at other times seem so horribly long to me—that I forget to tell you half of all that I had prepared in my imagination.

I wanted to ask you if the journey had not fatigued you, if the sea had been kind to you. I wanted to tell you all the admiration I feel for your noble character, for your incomparable devotion. More than one woman must have lost her mind amidst the repeated shocks of a lot so cruel, so undeserved.

I wanted to speak to you a long time of our children, of their health, their daily life. I wanted also to beg of you to thank all our families for their devotion to my cause—the cause of an innocent man—to ask you about their health. It would take a long day to exhaust all these subjects, and our minutes are numbered. Well, we must hope that the happy days are coming back to us, for it is impossible, it is contrary to human reason, to believe that they will not in the end put their hands upon the one who is really guilty.

As I have told you, I will do all in my power to conquer the beating of my sick heart, to bear this horrible and long martyrdom, so that I may live to see with you the happy light of the day of rehabilitation.

I will bear without a groan the natural scorn rightly inspired by the sight of the creature I represent. I will suppress the convulsions of my being against a lot so terrible, so appalling.

Oh, this scorn that shrouds my name, how it tortures me! My pen cannot express such suffering.

LETTERS OF AN INNOCENT MAN

I ask myself how a man who has really forfeited his honor can continue to live. But I live only because my conscience is clear, because I hope that soon all is to be discovered; that the true criminal will be punished for his odious crime, that they will at last give me back my honor.

When I am gone write me long letters. I am thinking of the moment when you all can write to me and when I shall receive news from all the members of our families.

The first time you are sending me anything, will you please send me the Ollendorf method which I have had a chance to try here, and which I think preferable to that of your teacher? Send with it the corrected exercises, which form a separate volume, and which will also be my teacher.

Embrace our darlings tenderly for me, your parents, all whom you see, and receive the affectionate kisses of your devoted   ALFRED.

1895—1896—1897—1898.

ILES DU SALUT.

Tuesday, 12 March, 1895.

My dear Lucie:

Thursday, the 21st of February, some hours after your departure, I was taken to Rochefort and put on shipboard.

I shall not speak to you of my voyage; I was transported in the manner in which the vile scoundrel whom I represent deserved to be transported. It was only just. They could not accord any pity to a traitor, the lowest of blackguards; and as long as I represent this wretch I can only approve their conduct.

My life here must drag itself out under the same conditions.

But your heart can tell you all that I have suffered—all that I suffer. I live only through the hope in my soul of soon seeing the triumphant light of my rehabilitation. That is the only thing that gives me strength to live. Without honor a man is not worthy of life.

On the day of my departure you assured me that the truth would surely come soon to light. I have lived during that awful voyage, I am living now, only on that word of yours—remember it well. I have been disembarked but a few minutes, and I have obtained permission to send you a cablegram.

I write in haste these few words, which will leave on the 15th by the English mail. It solaces me to have a talk with you, whom I love so profoundly. There are two mails a month for France—the 15th the English, and the 3d the French mail.

And in the same way there are two mails a month for the Isles—the English mail and the French mail. Find out the days of their departure and write to me by both of them.

All that I can tell you more is that if you want me to live have my honor given back to me. Convictions, whatever they may be, do nothing for me; they do not change my lot. What is necessary is a decision which will reinstate me.

I made for your sake the greatest sacrifice a man can make in resigning myself to live after my tragic fate was decided. I did this because you had inculcated in me the conviction that the truth must always come to light. In your turn, my darling, do all that is humanly possible to discover the truth. A wife and a mother yourself, try to move the hearts of wives and mothers, so that they may give up to you the key of this dreadful mystery. I must have my honor if you want me to live. I must have it for our dear children. Do not reason with your heart; that does no good. I have been convicted. Nothing can be changed in our tragic situation until the decision shall have been reversed. Reflect, then, and pursue the solution of this enigma. That will be worth more than coming here to share my horrible life. It will be the best, the only means of saving my life. Say to yourself that it is a question of life or death for me, for our children.

I am incapable of writing to you all. My brain will bear no more; my despair is too great. My nervous system is in a deplorable condition, and it is full time that this horrible tragedy should end.

Now my spirit alone is above water.

Oh, for God's sake, hurry, work with all your might! Tell them all to write to me.

Embrace them all for me; our poor darlings, too.

And for you a thousand tender kisses from your devoted husband, ALFRED.

When you have some good news to announce to me send me a dispatch. I am waiting for it day by day as for the Messiah.

---

15 March, 1895.

My Darling:

As I cannot send this letter until to-day I hasten to talk to you a little longer. I shall not speak of my appalling tortures; you know them and you share them with me.

My situation here is what it was before; be sure that I shall not be able to endure it long; it seems impracticable for you to come to join me. Moreover, as I told you yesterday, if you wish to save my life there is something better for you to do; have my honor given back to me—the honor of my name, the honor of the name of our poor children.

In my horrible distress I pass my time in mentally repeating the words you spoke the day of my departure—your absolute certainty of arriving at the truth. Otherwise it would be death for me, and that soon; for without my honor I could not live. I have surmounted everything only because of my conscience alone, and because of the hope you have given me that the truth will be discovered. Were this hope dead I, too, should die.

Say to yourself, therefore, my darling, that you must succeed, and that as soon as possible, in giving me back my honor. I cannot bear much longer this atmosphere of scorn, legitimate enough, which is all around me.

Upon your efforts depends my honor, and that is to say my life—the honor of our poor children, too. You must then attempt everything, try everything, to reach the truth, whether I live or die, for your mission has a higher object than my fate.

I embrace you as I love you.

ALFRED.

20 March, 1895.

My dear Lucie:

My letter will be short, for I do not wish to rend your soul; moreover, my sufferings are yours.

I cannot do more than repeat what I said in the letter that I wrote to you the 13th of this month. The more you hasten my rehabilitation the more you will abridge my martyrdom.

I have done for you more than the deepest love can inspire. I have endured the worst tortures to which a man of spirit can be subjected. Now it is your turn to do the impossible, to restore to me my honor, if you wish me to live.

My condition here is not yet definite; I am still in close confinement.

I will not speak to you of my material life, that is indifferent to me; physical miseries are nothing, whatever they may be. I wish for but one thing, and of that I dream night and day; with that my brain is always haunted; it is that they shall give me back the honor that never failed me.

As yet they have not given me the books that I brought; they are awaiting orders.

Always send me the reviews by the first post. Then, my darling, if you want me to live, have my honor given back to me as soon as possible; my martyrdom cannot be borne indefinitely. I think that I ought to tell you the truth rather than to calm you with deceitful illusions. We must look the situation in the face. I have been persuaded to live only because you have inculcated in my mind the conviction that innocence always makes itself known. My innocence must be made manifest not only for my sake, but for the children's, for you all.

Embrace the darlings, embrace every one for me, and a thousand kisses for yourself.

ALFRED.

LETTERS OF AN INNOCENT MAN

As letters will be very long in reaching me, send me a dispatch when you have good news to announce to me. My life hangs upon this expectation. Think of all that I am suffering.

---

28 March, 1895.

I was hoping to receive news of you at about this time; as yet I have heard nothing. I have already written you two letters.

I know nothing as yet beyond the four walls of my chamber. As for my health, it could not be very brilliant. Aside from my physical miseries, of which I speak only to cite them, the cause of this condition of my health lies chiefly in the disorder of my nervous system, produced by an uninterrupted succession of moral shocks.

You know that no matter how severe they might be at times, physical sufferings never wrung a groan from me, and that I could look death coolly in the face if only my mental sufferings did not darken my thoughts.

My mind cannot extricate itself for an instant from the horrible drama of which I am the victim, a tragedy which has struck a blow not only at my life—that is the least of evils, and truly it would have been better had the wretch who committed the crime killed me instead of wounding me as he has—but at my honor, the honor of my children, the honor of you all.

This piercing thought of my honor torn from me leaves me no rest either by day or by night. My nights, alas! you can imagine what they are! Formerly it was only sleeplessness, now the greater part of the night is passed in such a state of hallucination and of fever that

I ask myself each morning how my brain still resists. This is one of the most cruel of all my sufferings. Add to this the long hours of the day passed in solitary communion with my thoughts, in the most absolute isolation.

Is it possible to rise above such preoccupation of the mind? Is it possible to force the mind to turn aside to other subjects of thought? I do not believe it; at least I cannot. When one is in this, the most agitating, the most tragic, plight that can possibly be conceived for a man whose honor has never failed him, nothing can turn the mind from the idea which dominates it.

Then when I think of you, of our dear children, my grief is unutterable; for the weight of the crime which some wretch has committed weighs heavily upon you also. You must, therefore, for our children's sake, pursue without truce, without rest, the work you have undertaken, and you must make my innocence burst forth in such a way that no doubt can be left in the mind of any human being. Whoever may be the persons who are convinced of my innocence, tell yourself that they will change nothing in our position; we often pay ourselves in words and nourish ourselves on illusions; nothing but my rehabilitation can save us.

You see, then, what I cannot cease reiterating to you, that it is a matter of life or of death, not only for me, but for our children. For myself I never will accept life without my honor. To say that an innocent man ought to live, that he always can live, is a commonplace whose triteness drives me to despair.

I used to say it and I used to believe it. Now that I have suffered all this myself, I declare that if a man has any spirit he cannot live under such circumstances. Life is admissible only when he can lift his head and look the world in the face; otherwise, there is nothing left for him but to die. To live for the sake of living is simply low and cowardly.

I am sure that in this you think as I do; any other opinion would be unworthy of us.

The situation, already so tragic, becomes each day more tense. You have not to weep, not to groan, but to face it with all your energy and with all your soul. To make clear this situation, we must not wait for a happy chance, but we must display all-absorbing activity. Knock at all doors. We must employ all means to make the light burst forth. All forms of investigation must be tried; the object we have in view is my life, the life of every one of us.

Here is a very clear bulletin of my state, moral and physical. I will sum it up:

A pitiable nervous and cervical condition, but extreme moral energy, outstretched toward the one object, which, no matter what the price, no matter by what means, we must attain—vindication. I will leave you to judge from this what struggles I am each day forced to make to keep myself from choosing death rather than this slow agony in every fibre of my being, rather than this torture of every instinct, in which physical suffering is added to agony of soul. You see that I am holding to my promise that I made you to struggle to live until the day of my rehabilitation. It remains for you to do the rest if you would have me reach that day.

Then away with weakness. Tell yourself that I am suffering martyrdom, that each day my brain is growing weaker; tell yourself that it is a question of my honor—that is to say, of my life, of the honor of your children. Let these thoughts inspire you, and then act accordingly.

Embrace every one, the children, for me.

A thousand kisses from your husband, who loves you.

ALFRED.

How are the children? Give me news of them. I cannot think of you and of them without throbs of pain through my whole being. I would breathe into your soul all the fire that is in my own, to march forward to the assault that is to liberate the truth. I would convince you of the absolute necessity of unmasking the one who is guilty by every means, whatever it may be, and above all without delay.

Send me a few books.

---

27 April, 1895.

My dear Lucie:

A few more lines so that you may know that I am still living, and to send you the echo of my immense affection.

However great may be our grief, your grief and mine, I can only tell you always to surmount it in order to pursue the rehabilitation with indomitable perseverance.

Preserve at all times the calmness and the dignity which befit our misfortune, so great and so undeserved; but keep on working to restore to me my honor, the honor of the name which my dear children bear.

Let no setback rebuff you or discourage you; search out, if you think it useful, the members of the government, move their hearts, as fathers and as Frenchmen. Tell them that you ask for me no mercy, no pity, but only that the investigations may be absolutely thorough.

In spite of a combination of sufferings, physical as well as mental, which are at times terrible, I feel that my duty to you, to our dear children, is to resist to the limit of my strength and to protest my innocence with my last breath.

But if there is such a thing as justice in this world, it seems impossible to me, my reason refuses to believe, that we shall not recover the happiness which ought never to have been torn from us.

Truly, under the influence of extreme nervous excitement, or of a great physical depression, at times I write you feverish, excited letters; but who would not yield sometimes to such attacks of mental aberration, such revolts of the heart and soul, in a situation as tragic, as narrowing as ours? And if I urge you to hasten, it is because I long to be with you on that day of triumph when my innocence shall be recognized; and then when I am always alone, in solitude, given over to my sad thoughts, without news for more than two months of you, of the children, of all those who are dear to me, to whom should I confide the sufferings of my heart if not to you, the confidant of all my thoughts?

I suffer not for myself only, but yet more deeply for you, for our dear children. It is from them, my darling, that you must draw the moral strength, the superhuman energy which you need to succeed in making our honor appear again to every one, no matter at what price, what it has always been, pure and spotless.

But I know you. I know the greatness of your soul. I have confidence in you.

I am still without letters from you; as for me, this is the fifth letter that I have written. Kiss every one for me. A thousand fond kisses for you, for our dear children.

Tell me all about them.

ALFRED.

Wednesday, 8 May, 1895.

My dear Lucie:

Though I cannot send this letter before the 18th, I begin it to-day, so much do I feel the unconquerable need of talking with you.

It seems to me when I write to you that the distance is lessened. I see before me your beloved face and I feel that you are near me. It is a weakness. I know it; for in spite of myself the echo of my sufferings shows itself sometimes in my letters, and your sufferings are great enough without my continuing to tell you of mine. But I should like to see in my place the philosophers and psychologists who sit tranquilly in their chimney corners, offering their opinions upon the calmness and the serenity which should be shown by an innocent man.

A profound silence reigns around me, interrupted only by the roaring of the sea; and my thoughts, crossing the distance which separates us, carry me to your midst, among all those who are dear to me, whose thoughts must of a truth be often turned toward me. Often I ask at such an hour, "What is my dear Lucie doing?" and I send you by my thoughts the echo of my immense affection. Then I close my eyes, and it seems to me that I see your face and the faces of my dear children. I am still without letters from you, with the exception of those of the 16th and 17th of February, still addressed to the Ile de Ré. For three months now I have been without news of you, of the children, of our families.

I believe that I have already told you that I advised you to ask permission to leave your letters at the Ministry eight or ten days before the departure of the mails; perhaps in that way I shall receive them sooner. But, my good darling, forget all my sufferings, overcome your own, and think of our children. Say to yourself that you have a sacred mission to fulfill, that of having my honor given back to me, the honor of the name borne by our dear little ones. Moreover, I recall to my mind what you told me before my departure. I know, as you repeated to me in your letter of the 17th of February, what the words of your mouth are worth. I have an absolute confidence in you.

Then do not weep any more, my good darling; I will struggle until the last minute for you, for our dear children.

The body may give way under such a burden of grief, but the soul should remain firm and valiant, to protest against a lot that we have not deserved. When my honor is given back to me, then only, my good darling, we shall have the right to withdraw from the field. We will live for each other, far from the noise of the world; we will take refuge in our mutual affection, in our love, grown still stronger in these tragical events. We will sustain each other, that we may bind up the wounds of our hearts; we will live in our children, to whom we will consecrate the remainder of our days. We will try to make them good, simple beings, strong in body and mind. We will elevate their souls so that they may always find in them a refuge from the realities of life.

May this day come soon, for we have all paid our

tribute of sufferings upon this earth! Courage, then, my darling; be strong and valiant; carry on your work without weakness, with dignity, but with the conviction of your rights. I am going to lie down, to close my eyes and think of you. Good night and a thousand kisses.

---

12 May, 1895.

I continue this letter, for I wish to share with you all my thoughts as fast as they come into my mind. In my solitude I have the time to reflect deeply.

Indeed, the mothers who watch at the bedside of their sick children, for whom with ferocious energy they wrestle with death, have not so much need of a brave heart as have you; for it is more than the life of your children which you have to defend, it is their honor. But I know that you are fitted for this noble task.

So, my dear Lucie, I ask you to forgive me if at times I have added to your grief by my complainings, by showing a feverish impatience to see at last the light shining in upon this mystery, against which my reason battles in vain. But you know my nervous temperament, my hasty, passionate disposition. It seemed to me that all must be immediately discovered, that it was impossible that the truth should not be at once fully revealed. Each morning I arose with that hope and each night I went to my bed again a victim of the same deception. I thought only of my own tortures, and I forgot that you must suffer as much as I.

And this awful crime of some unknown wretch strikes not only at me, but it strikes also, and more than all, our two dear children. This is why we must conquer all our sufferings. It is not enough to give our children life; we must dower them with honor, without which life is not possible. I know your sentiments; I know that you think as I do. Courage, then, dear wife. I will struggle as you are struggling and sustain you with all my energy, because in the face of such an absolute necessity all else should be forgotten. We must, for the sake of our dear little Pierre, for the sake of our dear little Jeanne.

I know how marvellous you have been in your devotion, your grandeur of soul, in the tragic events just past.

Fight on, then, my dear Lucie. My confidence in you is absolute. My deep affection will recompense you some day for all the pains you are enduring so nobly.

---

18 May, 1895.

I am ending to-day this letter which will carry you a part of myself and the expression of the thoughts over which I have pondered deeply in the sepulchral silence that surrounds me.

I have thought too often of myself; not enough of you, of the children. Your suffering, that of our families, is as great as mine. Our hearts must be lifted high above it all, so that we shall see only the end which we must attain—our honor!

I will stand upright as long as my strength permits, to sustain you with all my ardor, with all the depth of my love.

Courage, then, dear Lucie—courage and perseverance. We have our little ones to defend.

Embrace our brothers and sisters for me; tell them that I have received the letters addressed to the Ile de Ré, and that I shall write to them soon.

For you my fondest kisses.

ALFRED.

I forgot to tell you that I received yesterday the two reviews of March 15, but nothing else.

Dear little Pierre:

Papa sends good big kisses to you, also to little Jeanne. Papa thinks often of both of you. You must show little Jeanne how to make beautiful towers with the wooden blocks, very high, such as I made for you, and which toppled down so well. Be very good. Give good caresses to your mamma when she is sorrowful. Be very gentle and kind also to grandmother and grandfather. Set good, little traps for your aunts. When papa comes back from his journey you will come to the railway station to meet him, with little Jeanne, with mamma, with every one.

More good big kisses for you and for Jeanne. Your

PAPA.

---

27 May, 1895.

My dear Lucie:

I profit by each mail to Cayenne to write to you, because I want to give you news of me as often as possible. During the month I wrote you a long letter. I sent it on the 18th.

Although I have not heard from you since my departure—all the letters having been dated earlier than our last interview—I am hoping that by the time that you receive this letter the denouement of our tragic story will be at hand.

However that may be, I cry to you always with all the strength of my soul: Courage and perseverance!

My nerves often get the better of me, but my moral energy remains unshaken; it is to-day greater than ever.

Let us, then, arm our hearts against every feeling of anxiety or grief; let us conquer our sufferings and our miseries, so that we may see nothing before us but the supreme object—our honor, the honor of our children! Everything should be effaced by that.

Then, still, courage, my dear Lucie. I will sustain you with all my energy, with all the strength that my innocence gives me, with all the longing that I have, to see the light shine out, full, perfect, absolute, as it must shine, for our sakes, for that of our children, of our two families.

Good kisses for the dear little ones.

I embrace you as I love you.

ALFRED.

---

3 June, 1895.

My dear Lucie:

Still no letters from you, nor from any one. Since my departure I have had no tidings of you, of our children, nor of any of the family.

You may have seen by my letters the successive crises through which I have passed. But for the moment let us forget the past. We will speak of our sufferings when we are happy again.

I do not know anything of what is passing around me, I live as in a tomb. I am incapable of deciphering in my brain this appalling enigma. All that I can do, then, and I shall not fail in this duty, is to sustain you to my last breath—is to continue to fan in your heart the flame which glows in mine, so that you may march straight forward to the conquest of the truth, so that you may get me back my honor, the honor of my children. You remember those lines of Shakespeare, in Othello. I found them again not long since among my English books. I send them to you translated (you will know why!).

> " Celui qui me vole ma bourse,*
>   Me vole une bagatelle
> C'est quelque chose, mais ce n'est rien.
> Elle était a moi, elle est à lui et,
>   A était l'esclave de mille autres.
> Mais celui qui me vole ma bonne renommée,
> Me vole une chose qui ni l'enrichit pas,
>   Et qui me rend vraiment pauvre."

Ah, yes! he has rendered me *"vraiment pauvre,"* the wretch who has stolen my honor! He has made us more miserable than the meanest of human creatures. But to each one his hour. Courage, then, dear Lucie; preserve the unconquerable will that you have shown until now; draw from your children the superhuman energy that triumphs over everything. Indeed, I have no doubt whatever that you will succeed, and I hope that this

---

*" Who steals my purse steals trash; 'tis something, nothing;
  'Twas mine, 'tis his, and has been slave to thousands!
  But he that filches from me my good name
  Robs me of that which not enriches him,
    And makes me poor indeed."

sinister tragedy is soon to end and that my innocence is at last to be recognized. What more can I tell you, my dear Lucie—what can I say that I have not told you in each one of my letters? My profound admiration for the courage, the heart, the character, that you have shown in such tragic circumstances; the absolute necessity, which supersedes everything, all interests, even our lives, of proving my innocence in such a way that not a doubt can remain in the mind of any one—the necessity of doing everything noiselessly, but with a determination that nothing can check.

I hope that you receive my letters; this is the ninth that I have written to you.

Embrace all the family; embrace our dear children for me, and receive for yourself the fondest kisses of your devoted   ALFRED.

As you see, my dear Lucie, I hope that when you receive these last letters the truth shall not be far from being known and that we shall enjoy again the happiness that was our lot until now.

---

11 June, 1895.

My dear Lucie:

Yesterday I received all your letters up to the 7th of March—that is to say the first which you addressed to me here—also the letter of your mother and the letters of your brothers and sisters, dating from the same time.

I wish to answer you while I am still under the spell of them. First of all I must speak to you of the immense joy I felt in reading the words written by your hand. It was something of yourself, a part of you, which had sought me out; it was your good, noble heart come to warm and revive mine.

I saw also in your letters what I had already felt—how you all have suffered in this horrible tragedy which has come upon us, surprising us in our happiness and tearing from us our honor. This one word tells everything, it sums up all our tortures—mine and yours.

I know that from the day when I promised you to live, to wait for the truth to be revealed, for justice to be done me, I ought not to have faltered. I ought to have silenced the voice of my heart; I ought to have waited patiently, but how could I? I had not the strength of soul.

The blow was too heavy. All within me revolted at the thought of the odious crime for which I had been condemned. My heart will bleed as long as this mantle of infamy weighs upon my shoulders.

But I ask you to forgive me if I have sometimes written you excited or complaining letters, that must have augmented your immense grief. Your heart and mine beat as one.

Be sure, then, my dear and good Lucie, that I shall resist with all my strength, so that I may reach the day when my happiness shall be given back to me. I hope that that day may come soon; until then we must look straight before us.

The news, too, you give me of our dear children has given me pleasure. Make them spend a great deal of time in the open air. Just now you must think only of giving them health and strength.

Courage then, still, dear Lucie; be strong and valiant. May my profound love sustain and guide you. My thoughts do not leave you for an instant, night or day.

Give news of me to all the family; thank them all for their good and affectionate letters. I have not the courage to answer them, and of what could I speak to them? I have but one thought, always the same—that of seeing the day when my honor shall be given back to me. I am always hoping that that day is near.

Embrace all your dear relations, the children, all our family, for me.

As for you, I embrace you with all the strength of my heart. ALFRED.

It is useless to send me anything in the way either of linen or of food. I received some preserves from Cayenne yesterday and I also asked for some linen which I need. They have given me the *Revue des Deux Mondes,* the *Revue de Paris,* and the *Revue Rose.* Continue to send them to me; you may also send a few light novels.

---

15 June, 1895, Saturday evening.

My dear Lucie:

I have already written to you, some days ago, on the receipt of your letters of the beginning of March, and my intention had been to send you, by this mail, only a few words of deep affection, for what can I tell you that I have not already told you again and again in all my letters? But in reading your dear letters, in re-reading them every day, I have felt each time I read them, for a moment, a lightening of my load of sorrow. It seemed to me that you were all near me and that I felt your hearts beating in sympathy with mine.

Sure that you have this same feeling, I yield to the impulse of my heart, which longs to do everything to bring some relief to your horrible sorrow. It is contrary to reason; I know it, for reason tells me to be calm and patient, that the light of truth will shine out, that it is impossible that it should be otherwise in the age in which we live; but yet when I write to you it is my heart that speaks, and then in spite of myself everything within me revolts against the appalling accusation so opposed to every feeling of our hearts, for to us honor is everything. I feel within me such a fever of combat, such power of energy to rend the impenetrable mantle that weighs me down, that still envelops this whole affair, that I am always longing to instill them into your souls, although I realize that the sentiments of you all are the same as my own. It is a useless outbreak, and I know it; but you know equally well that all my feelings are violent and deep. My heart bleeds for all that it holds most dear; it bleeds for you and it bleeds for our dear children, and that is to reiterate to you, my dear Lucie, that it is the longing I have to see the name you bear, that our dear children bear, once more as it has always been, pure, without a stain—it is this longing that gives me the strength to overcome all.

I live absorbed in myself. I neither see nor hear what passes around me. My brain alone still lives and all my thoughts are concentrated on you, on our dear children, on waiting until my honor is given back to me.

Then still hold to your splendid courage, my dear Lucie. I hope that we shall soon find the happiness which we used to enjoy and which we shall enjoy even more after this appalling trial, the most awful that a man can bear.

I embrace you with all my strength.   ALFRED.

LETTERS OF AN INNOCENT MAN

16 June, 1895, Sunday.

I continue my letter, always to the same end. Then, too, it is a happy moment for me when I come to talk with you; not that I have anything of interest to tell you, since I am living alone with my thoughts, but because, then, I feel that I am near to you. I can only tell you my thoughts just as they present themselves to me.

To-day a more peculiarly intimate sadness invades my soul, because on this day, Sunday, we used to be together all day and we used to end it with your dear parents. But my heart, my conscience, and my reason, too, tell me that these happy days will return to us. I cannot admit that an innocent man can be left to expiate indefinitely, for a guilty wretch, a crime as abominable as it is odious; and then, to sum it up in one word, what must give you, as it gives me, unconquerable energy, is the thought of our children, as I have already told you before, for ideas which emanate from such a subject must, from their nature, repeat themselves. We must have our honor, and we have not the right to be weak; without it, it would be better to see our children die.

As for our sufferings, we all suffer alike. Do you think that I do not feel what you suffer—you, who are struck doubly, in your honor and in your love? Do you believe that I do not feel how your parents suffer, your brothers and your sisters, for whom honor is not an empty word? But I hope that our anguish is to have an end, and that that end is near. Until that day we must guard all our courage, all our energy.

Thank Mathieu for those few words he wrote to me. How the poor boy must suffer; he who is honor incarnate! But tell him that I am with him in thought—that our two hearts suffer together. There are moments when I think that I am the plaything of a horrible nightmare; that all this is unreal; that it is only a bad dream; but it is, alas! the truth. But for the moment we ought to put aside every weakening thought. We ought to fix our eyes upon one single object: our honor. When that is returned to me, and when I know the meaning of what is now for me an unsolvable problem, perhaps I shall understand this enigma which baffles my reason, which leaves my brain panting.

I will wait, then, for that moment, sure that it will come. I wish for us all that it may come soon; I even *hope* it, so immovable is my faith in justice. Mystery has no place in our century. Everything is brought to light, and must be brought to light.

My Sunday has seemed less long to me, my dear Lucie, because in this way I have been able to talk with you. As for our children, I have no advice to give you. I know you; our ideas on this subject are alike, both in regard to their bringing up and in regard to their education. Courage always, dear Lucie, and a thousand kisses. Do not forget that I am answering letters dated three months ago, and that my replies may therefore seem out of date to you. ALFRED.

Friday, 21 June. 1895.

Dear Lucie:

I will continue our conversation, since it is now the only ray of happiness that we can enjoy. It is probable, and I hope it, that these reflections have nothing in common with the present state of affairs. Between the time when you will receive this letter and the date on which you wrote yours, there will be an interval of more than five months; in such a length of time the truth might well make great strides.

Like you, like you all, I am, I have been always, convinced that in time all will be discovered.

If I have wavered at times, it has been under the burden of atrocious moral suffering while anxiously waiting to know, at last, the solution of the riddle which absolutely baffles me.

You must understand through the feeling of reserve that keeps me from speaking to you on any aspect of my life here. Moreover, the only thoughts that agitate me are those that I tell to you; for the rest I live like a machine, unconscious of its movement.

It happens to me at times—and you, too, must feel this—when I am wide awake, and in spite of all that surrounds me, I stand bewildered, repeating to myself: " No, all that did not happen; it cannot be possible; it is a fiction; it is not reality!" I cannot explain to myself this passing inertia of the brain in any way other than by the impassable distance that lies between the innocence in my conscience and my present life. Nor can you picture to yourself what relief this long conversation with you brings to me. I dare not even read over my letter, so afraid am I to find in it repeatedly the same ideas expressed perhaps in exactly the same way; but for you, as for me, true pleasure consists in reading what the other has written.

When my heart is overburdened, when I am seized by the deep horror of it all, I draw new energy from your eyes, from the faces of our dear children. Your portrait, the portraits of the children here on my table, are always before my eyes. And then, you see, when a man has lost his fortune, when he has been subjected to some disappointment in his career, to a certain point he may indulge in weakness; he may say, "Well, my children will straighten all that out; perhaps it will be better for them than if they should have had nothing to do but be amiable idlers!" But in our case it is our honor which is at stake—their honor. To give way to weakness would be, for us, an unpardonable crime. We must, therefore, my dear and good Lucie, accept all our sufferings and overcome them, until the day when my innocence shall be recognized. On that day only we shall have the right to give free course to our tears, to unburden our hearts.

I am hoping, always, that that day may come soon. Each morning I awake with a new hope, and each night I lie down with a new disappointment.

I do not need to tell you that we can speak freely to each other of our grief—the fullest heart must sometimes overflow, but we must keep our outbursts to ourselves. I know, indeed, that you are sincere and singlehearted, without art of any kind. The fine qualities of your nature, those qualities which I, so to speak, only caught a fleeting glimpse of through our happiness, now stand out clear and distinct in the light of our adversity.

---

26 June, 1895.

I will to-day bring this long talk to an end, so that I may send off my letter. I should like to talk to you in this way morning and evening; but were I to write volumes, the same ideas would flow from my pen. Naturally active, in my solitude I am reduced to the necessity of coming constantly back to the same subject. The form alone might vary, according to the feeling of the moment, but the idea would remain the same because it dominates everything.

Give our dear children a fond embrace for me. I suppose that you will not keep them in Paris during the hot season. Let them take the initiative in a great part of their life; let them develop themselves freely and without constraint. In that way you will make virile beings of them. Finally, draw from them at the same time both consolation and strength.

Now I have only to tell you that I wish, that I am hoping always, that this sad drama is soon to end. That would be such a blessing for all, for us, as for our dear families.

Your poor, dear mother, even now so delicate; your dear father—they both will need rest and calm, after such appalling, such unimaginable tortures. We may well call them that.

Often and often I ask myself how you all are, when news of you is so rare, and comes from so far.

And how often I scan the horizon, my eyes turned toward France, hoping that this may be the day on which my country is to call me back to her. While we wait for that day let us stand firm, dear Lucie; let us draw from our consciences and from our duty, the fresh stores of the strength we need so much.

Embrace all our family for me, and for yourself the tenderest kisses of your devoted husband.

ALFRED.

2 July, 1895.

My dear Lucie:

When this letter reaches you your birthday will be at hand. The only hope that I can form, and which is in your heart as it is in mine, is that I shall soon be told that our honor is given back to us and with it our former happiness.

My conscience and my reason give me faith; the supernatural is not of this world. In the end everything is made clear. But the hours of waiting are long and cruel when the situation is so appalling as well for us as for our families.

Your dear letters of the beginning of March—you see how they are delayed—are my daily reading. I succeed thus, though far from you, in talking with you. My thoughts, indeed, never leave you, nor our dear children.

I await tidings of your health and that of our children with impatience. I am also anxious to know what date your letters will bear. My health is good. My heart beats with your own, and envelops you with all its tenderness. I have written you two long letters during the last half of June; I could only keep on repeating myself. Let me end this letter by embracing you with all the strength of our souls, and our dear children also.

Your devoted

ALFRED.

Kisses to all our family.

---

2 July, 11 o'clock in the evening.

My dear Lucie:

I had been without news of you since the seventh of March. This evening I received your letters of March and of the beginning of April; they, probably, had returned to France; then, later, those which you sent directly to the Ministry. I had already written a few words to you this morning, but I make haste to answer your letters by the same post.

Forgive me again if, by my first letters, I caused you pain. I ought to have hidden my atrocious sufferings from you. But my excuse is that there is no human grief comparable to that which we suffer.

I hope that you have received since then my many long letters; they must have reassured you as to my physical and mental condition. My conviction has never varied; it is founded in my conscience, and in my reason, which tells me that all will be found out. But I lacked patience.

Let us say no more of our sufferings. Let us simply do our duty, which is to restore to our children the honor of a father who is innocent of so abominable a crime.

I have received also letters bearing the same date from your dear parents, and from different members of our families. Embrace them for me and thank them. Tell Mathieu that my moral energy is as exalted as his own.

I embrace you with all my heart; also our dear children. Your devoted

ALFRED.

---

15 July, 1895.

My dear Lucie:

I wrote you so many and such long letters during the months when I did not hear from you that I have many times told and retold you all my thoughts, all my sorrows. Let me not return again to this last subject.

As for my thoughts, they are very clear to-day; they do not change; you know them.

My energy is occupied in stilling the beatings of my heart, in containing my impatience, to learn at last that my innocence is recognized everywhere and by every one. But if my energy is altogether passive, yours ought, on the contrary, to be all active and animated by the ardent spirit which gives strength to my own.

If it were merely a question of suffering it would be nothing. But it is a question of the honor of a name, of the life of our children, and I do not wish, you understand, that our children should ever have to lower their heads. Light, full, complete, must be let in upon this tragic story. Nothing, therefore, should rebuff or tire you. All doors open, all hearts beat for a mother who begs only for the truth, so that her children may live.

It is almost from the tomb—my situation here is comparable to that, with the added grief that my heart still beats—that I write these words to you. Thank your dear parents, our brothers and sisters, as well as Lucie and Henri, for their good and affectionate letters. Tell them all the pleasure which I take in reading them, and tell them that if I do not answer directly it is because I could do nothing but keep on repeating what I have already said. Kiss your dear parents for me; tell them all my affection. Long, tender kisses for the children. As for you, my dear and good Lucie, your letters are my daily reading. Continue to write me long letters; with them I come nearer to living with you, with our dear children, than I could by my thought alone, which, indeed, never leaves you for an instant.

I embrace you with all the strength of my soul.

               Your devoted   ALFRED.

LETTERS OF AN INNOCENT MAN

I have not received the things which you told me you were sending—that is to say, a sponge and some Kola-Chocolate. But do not give a thought to my material life; that is generously provided for by the preserves which are sent me from Cayenne.

---

27 July, 1895.

My dear Lucie:

I have already written to you on the 15th of the month. I can to-day give you tidings of myself, and cry to you as always, although I have no knowledge of the present state of affairs, " Courage and Faith ! "

My health is good. The spirit dominates the body, as it does everything else. Never will I admit the idea that it would be possible for our children to enter upon life with a dishonored name. It is from the inspiration of this thought, common to us both, that you ought to draw new life for your indomitable will.

I have never feared the future, but there are moral situations which are of such a character that if a man has not deserved them, he must of necessity escape from them as much for our own sake as for the sake of our children, of our families.

When a man asks, when he desires, nothing but the search for the truth, a search for the wretches who have committed the base and cowardly crime, he has a right to present himself everywhere with head erect. And this truth, it must be found, and you must find it. My innocence must be recognized by every one.

I want to be with you and with the children when that day comes.

LETTERS OF AN INNOCENT MAN

Kiss the dear little ones.
I live in them and in you.
I embrace you with all my heart.

Your devoted
ALFRED.

I hope to receive news of you before many days.

---

2 August, 1895.

My dear Lucie:

The mail from Cayenne arrived yesterday. I hoped to receive your letters as I did last month. This hope has been deferred. What shall I tell you, my dear and good Lucie, that I have not already said and repeated many times? If I have undergone the most shocking tortures, if I have borne up to this day a moral situation in which every instant is for me a wound, it has been because, innocent of that horrible treachery, I long for my honor—the honor of the name borne by our dear children.

Had I been alone in the world, probably, unable to have regained my honor for myself, I should have acted in another way.

Oh, in that case, I swear to you that I should have had the secret of this infernal machination. I should have left to the future the care of rehabilitating my memory. However incomprehensible to me this drama, in the end all would have been discovered—discovered naturally.

But there you were, there were our children, who bear my name, there was my family. I had to live to reclaim my honor, to sustain you by my presence, by all the ardor of my soul, for—and this thought is before all else—our children must enter life with heads erect. This patience of soul which is not mine, which I never can possess, I impose it upon myself, for it is my duty.

It is true, indeed, that I have had moments of horrible despair. All this mask of infamy that I wear for the wretch who is guilty burns my face, it crushes my heart; everything, in truth, all my being, revolts against a moral situation so absolutely opposed to what I am.

I do not know, my dear Lucie, what is the situation at the present hour, since your last letters were written more than two months ago; but no matter how the case now stands, say to yourself that a woman has all rights —sacred rights, if any are sacred, when she has to fulfill the highest mission which misfortune can force upon a wife and a mother.

As I have also often told you, you have to ask only for a thorough search for the truth. You ought certainly to find among those who direct the affairs of our country men of heart who will be moved by this bitter anguish of a wife and a mother, who will understand this awful martyrdom of a soldier for whom honor is everything. I cannot believe that everything will not be put in motion to help you in bringing the truth to light, to help you in unmasking the wretch, or the wretches, creatures unworthy of pity, who have committed this horrible treachery.

I can only give you the counsel which my heart suggests. You can appreciate better than I the means by which we may arrive at a prompt and complete rehabilitation.

But I may still say this, that the only thought which should now occupy your mind is this: the care of guarding the honor of the name you bear—this is to assure the life, the future of our children. This is the end necessary, and you must attain it, whatever may be the means. There must not remain one single Frenchman who doubts my honor.

Yours is a grand mission, and you are worthy to accomplish it. When honor shall be given back to us— and I hope for all our sakes it may be soon—I shall consecrate the remainder of my life to making you forget —yes, even you shall forget, my poor darling—these terrible months of pain and anguish; for, more than all others, you deserve to be happy and beloved for your great heart, for your wonderful strength of character.

Then, be always strong and valiant. May my spirit, my profound love, sustain and guide you.

My thoughts are constantly with you, with our dear little ones, with you all.

Kisses to the children—to all.

I embrace you with all my strength.

ALFRED.

---

2 August, 1895, 8 o'clock in the evening.

I had just ended this letter, so that it might leave to-morrow for Cayenne, when they brought me your letters of the month of April and your letters of June, with the letters of all the family. I have just read through your letters rapidly. I will answer at greater length by the next mail.

I have nothing to change in what I have just written to you. No matter how appalling to me the moral situation may be in which I am placed, no matter how my heart may be bruised, I shall stand erect to my last breath, for I want my honor, your honor, that of our children. As for my friends, I have never doubted them. They know what I am. But what is necessary, what I will have, is light, so brilliant that no one in all our dear country can have any doubt of my honor. It is my honor, the absolute honor of a soldier, that I must regain. This mission I confide to you, to you all. You will accomplish it, I have no doubt of it.

I embrace you; also our dear children.

Your devoted   ALFRED.

---

22 August, 1895.

My dear Lucie:

I wrote you two long letters at the beginning of the month, on the 2d and the 5th of August; I hope that both of them were in time to go by the English boat. It is a long time since I have had a talk with you. It was not the wish that I lacked. My whole heart is with you. How many times have I taken up my pen only to throw it aside! What does it profit us for me always to be stirring up these sorrows? Aside from your health, from the health of the children, that of all the family, I have only one thought—and that forces me to live—the thought of our honor.

You will forgive me if at times I have presented my ideas in a somewhat exaggerated form. But after all, if I do my duty, my whole duty, without flinching, it is not because my heart does not tremble and bleed in a situation so infamous and so undeserved, and its sorrow comes not only from my own situation, but from yours, from that of all whom I love.

And then remember that I am obliged to control myself night and day without one moment of respite, that I never open my mouth; that there is never a moment when my nerves are relaxed, so that when I write to you with my whole heart, everything that cries out in me for justice and truth runs, despite my will, under my pen.

But what I shall tell you always, as long as my heart shall beat, is that above all our sorrows, oh, however terrible they may be, before life itself, is honor, and that that honor, which belongs to us, must remain with us; it is the patrimony of our children. Then always and still again courage, Lucie, until we have seen the end of this horrible tragedy; but let us hope for all our sakes that it may come soon.

Kiss your dear parents, all of our family, for me. Tell them of my profound affection, and how often I think of them. As for you, my dear Lucie, I have no consolation to give you; there is none, either for you or for me, in such misfortune. But your conscience, the sense of the great duties which you have to fulfill, should give you invincible strength.

And then, when the day of justice dawns for us, we will find our consolation in our profound love.

A thousand kisses for you and for our dear children.

Your devoted

ALFRED.

---

27 August, 1895.

I add a few words before mailing this letter to send you again the echo of my profound affection, to tell you how much I thought of you on your birthday—hardly more, it is true, than on other days, that is not possible—

and to kiss you with all my heart and to say to you, "Courage and always courage!"

Ah, suffering, under all its forms, I know what it is, I swear to you. From the time that this trouble began my heart has been nothing but a wound which bleeds each day and every hour—a wound that will be healed only when I learn at last that my innocence is recognized. In truth, the mind stands at times bewildered and perplexed by the thought that such errors can be in a century like ours and can last so long without the light being let in upon them. But fear nothing; if I suffer beyond all expression, as you suffer, as you all suffer, indeed, my soul is still valiant, and it will do its duty to the end, for your sake, for the sake of our children. Ah, but let us hope that this appalling, this unbelievable situation may soon end, and that we may at last come out of the horrible nightmare in which we have been living for more than ten months!

Embrace our dear little ones tenderly for me.

---

7 September, 1895.

My dear Lucie:

I receive only to-day your letters of July, as well as those of all the family. I often do as you do. At certain moments when my full heart brims over, I re-read all your dear letters and I weep with you, for I do not believe that two beings who place honor above everything, and with them their families, have ever undergone a martyrdom like ours. I suffer, and, like you, like you all, I am not ashamed of it. My heart, night and day, demands its honor, yours, the honor of our children.

Such a situation is tragic, the anguish becomes too great for us all to bear.

Should it last much longer either one or the other will give way under it. Well, my dear Lucie, that must not be! We must before all else get back our honor, the honor of our children. We must not allow ourselves to be overcome by a fate so infamous when it is so unmerited. However natural, however legitimate, may be the cries of pain of souls who suffer far beyond all imaginable suffering, to groan, my dear Lucie, will do no good. If, when you receive this letter, the mystery has not been made clear, then, I think, it will be time, with the courage, the energy which duty gives, with the invincible force which innocence gives, for you to take personal steps, so that at last light may be thrown upon this tragic story. You have neither mercy nor favor to ask for, but only a determined search for the truth, a search for the wretch who wrote that infamous letter, and, in one word, justice for us all! And you will find in your own heart words more eloquent than any that could be contained in a mere letter. We must, in a word, find at last the key to this mystery. Whatever may be the means, your position as a wife and a mother gives you every right and should give you every courage.

From what I myself feel from the state of my own heart, I know but too well how it must be with you all, and in my long nights I see you suffering, agonizing with me.

It must end. Men cannot in a century like ours leave two families in agony without clearing up a mystery like this. The truth can be made known, if only they are willing to have it so. Then, my dear Lucie, while you continue to preserve the dignity which must never abandon you, be strong, courageous, energetic! Whether great or humble, we are all equal before justice, and that honor which I have never forfeited, and which is the patrimony of our children, must be given back to us. I want to be with you and with our children when that day comes.

Kisses to all. I embrace you with all my strength, also our dear children.

Your devoted
ALFRED.

---

7 September, evening.

Before sending this away so that it may leave by the English boat I want to add a few words; all my heart, all my thoughts, are with you and with our dear children.

I have just re-read your dear letters, and I need not tell you that I shall read them often until the next mail brings me others. The days are long when one is alone, face to face with one's thoughts, never speaking a word.

May my soul inspire you, my dear Lucie, for I feel that for the sake of your dear parents, for the sake of all of us, this tragedy must end. Even if you should have to knock at all doors, we must find the clue to this enigma, this infernal machination, which has torn from us that which makes life itself, and that we must have— our honor.

As for our dear children, kiss them with all your heart for me. The few words which Pierre adds to each letter give me great pleasure. It is for you and for them that I have found the strength to bear all, and

LETTERS OF AN INNOCENT MAN

I long to live to see the day when honor shall be returned to us. I wish for this with all my strength, with all my power, with all the energy of a man who places honor above all else. May this wish soon be realized! You must do all in your power to accomplish it.

I embrace you again, with all my heart.

Your devoted

ALFRED.

Kiss your dear parents and all our family for me.

---

27 September, 1895.

My dear Lucie:

For nearly a year I have struggled with my conscience against the most inexplicable fatality that can pursue a man.

There are times when I am so harassed, so disgusted, that I am like the soldier who, worn out by long-continued fatigue, lies down in a trench, longing to have done with life.

My soul awakes, the sense of my duty puts me on my feet again, all my being then nerves itself for a supreme effort, for I wish to find myself again with you and with my children on the day when my honor shall be returned to me.

But it is truly an agony that is renewed with every day, a punishment as horrible as it is unmerited.

If I tell you all this, if at times I have allowed you to catch a glimpse of how horrible is my life here, how this lot of infamy, whose effects continue day by day to harrow my being, to revolt my heart, it is not that I would complain; it is to tell you again that if I have lived, if I continue to live, it is because I desire my honor, yours, that of our children. May your spirit, your energy, rise equal to such tragic conditions, for this must come to an end.

This is why I told you in my letter of the 7th of September that if when you receive these letters the mystery is not made entirely clear, it is for you, for you personally, to go to the public authorities, so that light may at last be thrown on this tragic story.

You have the right to present yourself everywhere, with your head erect, for you have come not to beg for mercy, not to beg for favors, not even for moral convictions, however legitimate they may be. You have come to demand the search for the discovery of the wretches who have committed the infamous and cowardly crime. The Government has all the means by which this may be done.

Letters can do nothing, dear Lucie. It is you yourself who must act. What you have to say will receive from your lips a power, a force, that paper and writing cannot give.

Then, my dear Lucie, strong in your conscience, in your quality of wife and mother, go on your way, tireless until justice is done to us. And this justice, which you must demand energetically, resolutely, with all your soul, is that light may be thrown, full and unshadowed, upon this machination of which we are the wretched victims.

But you know what you have to say, and you must say it squarely, proudly.

Yes, my dear Lucie, that was what I thought from the first. I should, without making any noise about it, without any go-between except the person introducing me, have taken a child by each hand, and I should have gone to demand justice everywhere, without resting until the guilty wretches should have been unmasked. These means are "heroic," but they are the best means, for they come from the heart, and they appeal to the heart, to that sense of justice that is innate in each one of us, unless he is carried away by passion. They proceed from the strength given by innocence, from a duty to be fulfilled; and they know no obstacle. They are means worthy of a woman who asks only for justice for her husband, for her children.

It must not be said that in our century a wretch can with impunity crush the lives of two families.

Courage, then, dear Lucie, and act with resolution. Kisses to all. I embrace you with all my strength, and our dear, adored children.

Your devoted
ALFRED.

Since the package of June last I have received neither books nor reviews. I thought that you would continue to send me books and reviews each month regularly. Think of my perpetual tête-à tête with myself. I am more silent than a Trappist Monk, in my profound isolation, a prey to sad thoughts, upon a lonely rock, sustaining myself only by the force of duty.

---

4 October, 1895.

My dear Lucie:

I have just received your dear letters of August, so impatiently waited for each month, and with them the letters of all the family. Always write long letters to me. I feel a childish pleasure in reading what you have written, for then it seems to me that I hear you speak, that I feel the beating of your heart close to mine.

When you suffer too much take your pen and come and talk with me.

I thank you for your good tidings of the children. Kiss them tenderly for me.

My body, dear Lucie, is indifferent to everything; it is fortified by a strength almost superhuman, by a higher power—the anxiety, desire for our honor.

It is the sacred duty which I must fulfill—my duty to you, to our children, to our families—which fills my soul and rules it, which silences my broken heart. Were it not for that the burden would be too heavy for human shoulders.

Enough of moaning, Lucie; it will not make things any better. This appalling suffering must end for us all.

Strong in my innocence, march straight onward to your goal; silently, quietly, but openly and energetically, even if you are forced to carry your cause before the highest heads. No human heart can remain insensible to the supplications of a wife who comes with her little children to ask that the guilty be unmasked, that justice be done to the miserable, wretched victims. Do not look back over the past, but speak from your heart, from your whole heart; this tragedy of which we are the victims is poignant enough even in its simplicity.

Act, then, as I advised you in my letters of the 7th and 27th of September, frankly, resolutely, with the spirit of a woman who has to defend the honor—that is to say, the life—of her husband, of her children.

Do not give way to grief, my dear and good Lucie;

that will not help us. Pass from words to acts, and become great and worthy by those acts.

Embrace your dear parents and all our family for me. Thank them for their good, affectionate letters; thank also your dear aunt for the touching lines she has written to me. I do not write to them directly, though my heart night and day is with them all; for I could only go on repeating myself.

Courage, then, dear Lucie; we must see the end of this tragedy.

I embrace you with all my strength, with all my soul, and also our dear children.

Your devoted

ALFRED.

The books you have sent me have been announced, but I have not yet received them. I thank you; I had great need of them, for reading is the only thing which can distract my thoughts a little.

---

5 October, 1895.

My dear Lucie:

I had already written to you yesterday, but after I had read and re-read all the letters from this last mail there arose from them such a cry of agony that all my being was profoundly shaken.

You suffer for me, and I suffer for you.

No, it is not possible, it cannot be that an entire family can be subjected to such martyrdom.

Merely from the agony of waiting, we shall all be brought to the ground. It must not be; there are our children; they must be thought of before all else. I have just written again directly to the President of the Republic. I can act only by my pen—it is very little—I can only sustain you by all the ardor of my soul. You must, on your side, act energetically, resolutely. When a man is innocent, when he asks for nothing but justice, the clearing up of this terrible mystery, he is strong, invincible.

Lay, if need be, our dear children at the feet of the President, and demand justice for them, for their father.

Be heroic in your deeds, dear Lucie; it is on you that this duty falls.

Yet once more I must say it; it is not noise nor gnashing of teeth that is necessary, but an indomitable will, that nothing can rebuff.

I sustain you, from here, across all the distance, with all the living force of my being, with my soul of a Frenchman, of an honest man, of a father who demands his honor—the honor of his children.

I embrace you from the depths of my heart.

Your devoted

ALFRED.

26 October, 1895.

My dear Lucie:

I can do little but confirm my letters of the 3d and the 5th of October, and that of the 27th of September. We are both wearing out our strength while we wait in a situation as terrible as it is undeserved, and it will end by failing us, for all things have their limit. But there are our children, to whom we owe ourselves, who must have their honor before anything else.

That is why, trembling with anguish, not only on account of all that we have both suffered so long, nor this martyrdom of a whole family, I have written to the President of the Republic. I have written you my last letters to tell you that you must act, carrying out your purpose unflinchingly, with the head proudly raised, as innocent people who beg neither for mercy nor for favors, but only for light and justice. Even if one may bow the head under certain misfortunes, never can a man accept dishonor when he has not merited it.

Our suffering has no place in this epoch; it has lasted long enough—too long. Energy, then, my dear Lucie, the energy of work, of action, which must triumph, for it is based on justice, for it asks nothing but light, the clear light of day, the absolute clearing up of this whole affair. We are not in the presence of an unsolvable mystery. As I have told you, not tears, not words, but acts, are necessary.

The honor of a man, of his children, of two families, is in the balance, and it outweighs all passions, all interests. Act, then, my dear Lucie, with the heroic courage of a woman who has a noble mission to accomplish, even should you have to carry the question everywhere—before the highest heads; and I hope soon to hear that this appalling agony is to come to an end.

Kisses to all.

I embrace you and our dear children with all the force of my affection.

ALFRED.

26 October, 1895, evening.

Before I send this letter I want to add a few words, for thus it seems to me that I come near you and talk with you as in those happy times when we chatted together in our chimney corner. And, then, these are the only moments when I say a word, and if I were to listen only to my desire, I should talk so with you every day, and every hour in the day—but I should always say the same words.

If at times I groan, it is that being such as you know me to be—and you know that I am neither patient nor resigned—the anguish is too great, the hours weigh too heavy on my soul. I do not pretend to be stronger than I am. If I do succeed in holding out I have told you why. I do not want to return to it. But if I am reduced to mere groaning, if I must stand with folded arms before the most appalling sorrow that the honest and ardent heart of a soldier can feel when he is struck not only in himself, but in his wife, his children, in those he loves, I say to you yourself, as I say to you all, "Courage, individual energy!" When a man is subjected to a misfortune so undeserved he conquers it; and he does not conquer it by tears, or by recriminations, but by going straight forward. Our goal is our honor, and we should press forward with active, indefatigable energy, an energy that should be as great as the circumstances that exact our effort.

After all, there is a justice in this world, and it is not possible that the innocent should remain subjected to such martyrdom. Yes, I am repeating myself, and I can do nothing but repeat myself. My opinions have not changed. All this is rather that I may chat a little with you than for any other reason; to pass with you an hour of our long nights, for, as I have told you, I am now awaiting the result of your efforts and of the steps you have taken, which I think will not now be long delayed; and I am hoping that I shall soon see the day when I can breathe freer, when I can relax myself a little; it is full time, of that I assure you.

I send more fond kisses for you and for the children.
ALFRED.

---

4 November, 1895.

My dear Lucie:

The mail coming from Cayenne has arrived, and it has not brought me any letters. I have now been without tidings of you, of the children, since the 25th of August, but I will not let the English mail leave without writing you a few words. I shall not be long, for grief makes my pen tremble in my fingers.

I think, my dear Lucie, that you are now in possession of my last letters, and that you yourself are acting with the heroic spirit of a woman; that you are demanding the truth on every side; that you are demanding justice for miserable victims; that each day is a day thus employed until that on which the light breaks, until our honor is returned to us.

I think, therefore, that I shall soon learn that this appalling agony is at last at an end. I need not remind you to ask permission to send me a dispatch when you shall have good news to tell.

The days are long, the hours are heavy, when one has suffered so, and for so long a time.

I embrace you with all my strength, and the children, too. Your devoted
ALFRED.

Kisses to all.

LETTERS OF AN INNOCENT MAN

20 November, 1895.

My dear Lucie:

On the 11th I received your dear, good letters of September, as well as letters from all the family. I need not tell you the intense joy I felt in reading words from you.

I thank you for remembering my birthday. I will not speak of it further, for we must not linger over sad memories. What we need now, as you have said so truly, is reality, the truth. After one has suffered in a manner so atrocious and for so long a time, one's energies, one's activity, above all, ought to grow in proportion to the sufferings which one endures. Strong in your conscience, it is your right, I will even say it is your duty, to attempt all, to dare all, in order to throw light upon this tragic story, to regain at last our honor, the honor of our children.

As I have told you, in this situation, as horrible as it is undeserved, which would soon crush us, there no longer can be any thought of waiting for some happy chance, such as we have already waited for too long.

You have now received my letters of October. You ought to act with the force given by my innocence, with the power inspired by the knowledge that you have a noble mission to fulfill.

If I have told you to ask to have this matter cleared up by every, if even by heroic means, it is because there are situations which, when they are undeserved, are too much to be endured, which we must put an end to. You know that your soul and mine are but one; they throb together; and what I have told you must certainly have made yours tremble and throb.

So I am now waiting for the end of this awful drama, and I count the days.

LETTERS OF AN INNOCENT MAN

Thanks for the good news that you give me of the children. Kiss them fondly for me until I can embrace them for myself.

My tenderest kisses for you.

From your devoted
ALFRED.

Embrace your dear parents, all our family, for me.

I do not know by what route you sent the books and the reviews that you spoke of in your letters of the 25th of August, but they certainly have not yet arrived at Guiana.

---

27 December, 1895.

My dear Lucie:

I have not yet received your dear letters of October. Neither the French mail of November nor the English mail of December has brought them. What does it mean? What ought I to think of it? In what horrible nightmare have I lived for almost fifteen months?

As for suffering, alas! my poor darling, we both know what that is; and besides that, sufferings are of little importance, no matter what they are. What you must have is our honor, the honor of our children.

I wrote you a long letter on the 2d of December. To add anything to that letter, or, indeed, to any that preceded it, would be superfluous, would it not? Our thoughts are the same; our hearts have always beaten as one; our souls thrill together to-day, and they cry out for their honor with the burning ardor of honorable hearts struck in all that they hold most precious.

I wait with feverish impatience for news of you. I feel sure that it will soon arrive. I will even say that nearly every day I expect good news. I hope at last to hear something certain, positive, that the light has broken, or, at least, is soon to break, upon this bitterly sad story.

Let me tell you to-day simply that the thought of you, of our dear children, alone gives me the force to live through these long days, these interminable nights.

I embrace you with all my strength, as I love you, and our dear, adored children.

Your devoted
ALFRED.

Kisses to your dear parents, to all our family.

Again for long months I have received neither books nor reviews. Those that you told me of in your letter of August have not yet arrived. I cannot understand it.

I thought that you would have continued to send me regularly each month the reviews and a few packages of books, by mail. I am all day long, and I may add, nearly all night long, without a minute of forgetfulness, looking at the four walls of my cabin—well, it is of little importance, but it would be well to inquire what has become of these books.

---

31 December, 1895.

My dear Lucie:

I wrote to you some days ago to tell you that I had not yet received your letters of October. At last, after a long and terrible time of waiting, I have just received your letters of October, and at the same time those of November.

How must I sometimes cause you pain by my letters,

my poor darling, and you suffer so much without that! But at times it is stronger than I am, so eager am I to see the end of this horrible drama, for I would willingly give my blood, drop by drop, to learn at last that my innocence is recognized, that the guilty ones, doubly criminal as they are, are unmasked.

But when I suffer too much, when I faint before this life of deluding memories, of restraint of all my intellectual and physical forces, I murmur to myself the three names that are my talisman, that make me live on —yours, those of our dear little Pierre, and Jeanne.

Let us hope that we shall soon see the end of this awful drama. I cannot write much to you, for what can I tell you that is not already common to us? I live in the thought of you, and my soul is with you from morning till night, and from night till morning. All my faculties are straining toward the end that must be attained, that you will attain—all my honor as a soldier, all the honor of our children.

Perhaps I give you extravagant advice at times, the issue of the dreams of a lonely exile who is suffering martyrdom, a martyrdom whose tortures are made up not only of his own anguish, but of yours, of the anguish you all suffer . . . and nevertheless I know perfectly well that you can judge far better than I can of the means to attain my complete, my absolute, rehabilitation. I am going to pass a good part of the night, of the long, long days in reading and re-reading your dear letters, in living with you, in sustaining you in my thoughts with all my strength, with all my ardor, with all the force of my will.

My health is good; do not be anxious on that score. Moreover, to reassure you, I have asked permission to send you a dispatch. I trust that it will reach you. I hope that your health, that the health of you all, is also good. You must sustain yourself physically to have the force necessary to arrive at the goal.

Let us hope that soon, near to one another and with our dear children at our side, we may forget the events of this horrible tragedy. You must all tell yourselves, too, that if at times I cry out in anguish, it is because I am always as silent as the dead. I have only the paper, and these cries of grief, these cries of suffering—call them what you will—my heart is always valiant, even if it cannot always be silent. So I am waiting just as you asked me to, and I will wait until that day when the light shall at last shine out.

Long and tender kisses to our dear children. I often gaze at their portraits and I try to see them as they are to-day.

Ah, dear Lucie, remember that in my moments of distress I have these three names, that are my support, my safeguard, that raise me when I fall, for our children must enter upon life with heads erect.

I embrace you as I love you, with all my strength.

ALFRED.

---

3 January, 1896.

My dear Lucie:

I read and re-read with eagerness your dear letters of October and November, and although I have written to you already, on the 31st of December, I want to come again and talk with you.

Your letters could not increase my affection, but they

inspire in me an admiration, each day increasing, of your character, your great heart, and I am ashamed of myself for not knowing better how to suffer, for sometimes writing you such nervous, such disquieting letters. As to our purpose I have never wavered. I am innocent, and my innocence must shine out. Our name must again become what it deserves to be. But you must understand that my torments are at times so sharp, the revolt of my heart is at times so violent, that I cry out in spite of myself; it seems that, no matter at what cost, I must learn the secret of this infamy, must make the truth break forth, make justice triumph.

I have never been discouraged, I have never doubted that a will strong in its innocence and in the duty it has to accomplish could fail to attain its object. I have had, perhaps may again have, attacks of febrile impatience, the revolts of an ardent spirit, that has for so long been crushed under foot, weighed down by this sepulchral silence, this enervating climate, the frequent absence of news, nothing to do, and often nothing to read. But if the tension of my nervous system was extreme during the last three months of 1895—that was the hottest season, the worst season in Guiana—my courage never weakened, for it was it that held me up, that permitted me to double the dangerous cape without flinching. Do not lay any stress upon this nervousness which breaks out at times. Tell yourself that I am determined to be with you, at your side, on the day when honor shall be given back to us.

Your will, the will of you all, must continue to be what it has always been, as great, as unconquerable as it is calm and thoughtful.

My health is good; my body, indifferent to everything, animated by but one thought, common to us all, common, as your dear mother has said, to this whole sheaf of hearts, quivering with pain, lives for the honor so unjustly wrested from us.

And remember that if I at times have moments of personal weakness, under the repeated shocks of this trying hour, I have also a talisman, to reanimate me, to give me strength, the thought of you, of my children—in a word, my duty.

The lines in which you speak to me of the dear children give me great pleasure; they permit me to see the children in my thoughts.

Embrace the darlings tenderly for me.

So, my dear and good Lucie, courage always. Hold your head proudly high until the day comes when, side by side, we can forget this horrible drama.

Let us hope for all our sakes that that hour may be at hand.

I embrace you as I love you.

Your devoted

ALFRED.

Kisses to all.

---

26 January, 1896.

You ask me, my dear and good Lucie, to write you long letters. What can I tell you that you do not feel in your own heart better than I could tell it? My heart is always with you; it is torn when it feels you suffer pangs so unmerited, and can do nothing to help you, except to suffer equally itself. My spirit night and day is with you; it would sustain and animate you with its ardent fervor. I can only repeat what I have so often said, the end is everything; the honor of our name, the honor of our children; and that must be attained against all obstacles, in spite of everything. But the situation is so atrocious, as well for you as for me, that our activities, which should be of every kind, as they should be of every hour, far from weakening, ought, on the contrary, to grow still stronger and tax their ingenuity to the utmost in order to succeed in making the truth shine in all its brilliancy.

My health is good. I continue to struggle against everything so that I may be there with you, with our children, on the day when my honor is given back to me. I hope ardently, for your sake as for mine, that that day may not be too long delayed.

I expect to receive news of you in a few days, and as always, I am waiting for it with feverish impatience. I shall write to you more at length when I shall have received your letters.

Kiss both the children many, many times for me. Their dear little letters, like yours, like the letters from all our friends, are my daily reading.

I need not tell you the thrill of happiness they give. And for yourself the best, the tenderest kisses of your devoted　　　　　　　　　　　　　　　　　ALFRED.

---

5 February, 1896.

My dear Lucie:

The mail has arrived, and it has brought me no letter. I need not tell you what bitter disappointment. I could tell you what deep grief I feel when this only consolation, your dear beloved words, do not come to me. But, as I have said before, of what importance are sufferings —I dare even call them tortures—however atrocious, however horrible they may be, for the object which you are now pursuing dominates everything, it is above all else, and beyond all else—the honor of our name, the honor of our dear, adored children.

As for me, dear Lucie, you are my strength, my invicible strength, so high are you in my love, in my tenderness. Like my children, you dictate to me my duty. Say to yourself that if often the violence of feelings, that are at times atrocious, wrings a groan from my heart and makes my brain reel; if at times the unending hours and the climate exceed my strength of forbearance, and my very flesh cry out, my determination remains unshaken.

But you must realize all that I suffer on account of your martyrdom, from the unmerited dishonor cast upon our children, upon all our family. You must feel all that I suffer from such a condition of soul, striving here against many elements united; what a determination, what a power I feel within me to see the light—oh, no matter at what price, no matter by what means! Often in this solitude the tempest rages in my brain; oftener yet the blood boils in my veins with impatience to see the end of this incredible martyrdom. The more atrocious my sufferings the more they increase as the days roll by, the less willing we should be to give way to grief or to rebuffs, the less inclined we should be to give ourselves over to fate. And since our tortures are to cease only after the light dawns full and entire, and since we must have it through and against everything for ourselves, for our children, for us all, our wills should strengthen as difficulties and obstacles increase. Therefore, dear and good Lucie, courage, and more than courage; a strong will, a daring will that knows how to be determined and to succeed, a will strong enough to attain its object, no matter how, an object as praiseworthy as it is elevated—the truth. This has lasted too long, too many sufferings are crushing down innocent beings.

Kiss the dear children often and fondly for me. Ah, indeed, dear Lucie, there is nothing that can be called an obstacle where our children are concerned. Remind yourself that there are no obstacles; that there cannot be any; that the truth must be known; that a mother has all rights, as she ought to have all courage when she is called upon to defend that by which alone her children can live—their honor.

And each time when I write to you I cannot bring myself to close my letter, so brief is this moment when I come to talk to you; so wholly is all my being with you; so entirely all I say fails to express the feelings that agitate me and fill my soul; so inadequate to express this desire, stronger than all else, which is in me—a desire for the truth and for our honor and the honor of our children, or to express my deep love for you, my love increased by unbounded reverence.

I hope, indeed, that what I have said to you during so many long months is being translated by you all into strong and vigorous action, and that I shall hear soon that the sufferings of us both are to have an end.

I embrace you as I love you, and also our dear children, with all my heart, with all my soul, while I wait for tidings from you all.

ALFRED.

LETTERS OF AN INNOCENT MAN

26 February, 1896.

My dear Lucie:

I received the 12th of this month your dear letters of December; also all those from the family. It is needless for me to try to describe to you the deep emotion which they gave me. I could weep—that tells it all. As you yourself feel, in spite of yourself, the brain does not stop working, the head and the heart still suffer, and these tortures will only cease after the truth is brought to light, when this awful drama is finished, explained.

I have spoken too much of myself and of my sufferings; forgive me this weakness.

Whatever my sufferings may be, ah, however terrible our martyrdom is, there is an object that must be attained—that you will attain, I am sure of it—the light, full and entire, such as is necessary for us all, for our name, for our dear children. I hope ardently, for you as for myself, to hear soon that this object is at last attained.

I have no counsels to give you, either. I can but approve absolutely what you are doing to accomplish the complete demonstration of my innocence. That is the end to be attained, and we must see nothing else.

I have received Mathieu's few words; tell him that I am always with him, heart and soul. The 22d of February was the anniversary of the birth of our dear little Jeanne. How often I thought of her! I will not say more about it, for my heart will break and I have need of all my strength. Write me long letters. Speak to me of yourself and of our dear children.

I read and re-read each day all that you have written me; then it seems to me that I hear your beloved voice, and that helps me to live.

I will not write more, for I can only tell you of the horrible length of the hours, of the sadness of all things; and complaining is very useless.

Kiss your dear parents for me. Thank them always for their good, affectionate letters.

A thousand kisses to our dear children, and for you the best, the tenderest kisses of your devoted

ALFRED.

I have not yet received the things you spoke of in your letters of the 25th of November and the 25th of December. I cannot tell why the things you send me are so long in coming. Perhaps the books you are going to send me soon by mail will reach me with less delay. I hope so, for reading, the only thing that is possible for me to do, may calm a little the pains in my brain, and unhappily even that is often lacking.

---

5 March, 1896.

My dear Lucie:

I have not yet received your dear letters of January. A few lines only to send you the echo of my immense affection. Write to you at length? I cannot. My days, my hours, slip by monotonously, in this agonizing, enervating waiting for the discovery of the truth, the discovery of the wretch who committed this infamous crime. Speak to you of myself? What good can that do us? My sufferings, you know them, you share them. They, like yours, like those of all who love us, can only have an end when the broad, full light shall appear, when honor is returned to us.

It is toward this end that all your energy, all your

forces, all your means, should be directed. I hope to learn that this end is almost attained, that this appalling martyrdom of a whole family is nearly over. My body, my health? All that is indifferent to me. My being is animated only by one thought, by one desire, which keeps me alive—that of seeing with you and with our children the day when my honor shall be returned to me. It is in my thoughts of you, in the thought of our adored children, that I rest my brain, overtried at times by this continual tension, by this fever of impatience, by this terrible inactivity, without one moment of distraction.

If, then, we cannot keep ourselves from suffering—for never were human beings, who hold honor above all, struck in such a manner—still I cry always to you, "Courage, courage!" to march on to your goal, your head high, your heart firm, with unshaken will, never discouraged. Your children tell you your duty, just as they give me my strength.

Let us hope, then, as your mother has said, that soon, in each other's arms, we can try to forget this fearful martyrdom, these months, so sad and so delusive, and live again by consecrating ourselves to our children.

I embrace you, as I love you, with all my strength, and also our dear children.

Your devoted   ALFRED.

Kisses to all.

---

26 March, 1896.

My dear Lucie:

I received the 12th of this month your good letters of January, so impatiently expected every month, also all the letters from the family.

LETTERS OF AN INNOCENT MAN

I have seen with happiness that your health and the health of all resist this frightful condition of things, this horrible nightmare, in which we have lived so long. What a trial for you, my good darling, as horrible as it is undeserved—for you who deserve to be so happy! Yes, I have horrible moments, when the heart can bear no longer the blows which open the wound already so deep, when my brain gives way under the weight of thoughts so sad and so deceptive. When, after I have waited for my letters in an agony of anxiety, the mail arrives, and still I do not receive the announcement of the discovery of the truth, or of the author of that infamous and cowardly crime, oh, I have at first a feeling of deep, bitter disappointment. My heart is torn, is broken, under so many sufferings, so long and so undeserved!

I am a little like a sick man who lingers on his bed of torment, suffering anguish, but who lives because his duty demands it, and who keeps asking his doctor, "When will my tortures end?" And as the doctor answers, "Soon, soon," the sick man ends by asking himself, "But when will this 'soon' come?" and he longs to see it come.

It was a long time ago that you announced it to me . . . but be discouraged? Oh, that never! However terrible may be my sufferings, the desire for our honor is far above them!

Neither you, nor any one, will ever have the right to one moment of fatigue, one second of weakness, as long as the goal has not been reached—the absolute honor of our name. As for me, when I feel that I am falling under the united weight of all our suffering, when I feel that my reason is leaving me, then I think of you, of our dear children, of the undeserved dishonor cast upon our name, and I recover my balance by a violent effort of my whole being, and I cry to myself, "No, you shall not bend before the tempest! Your heart may be in bits, your brain may be crushed, but you shall not succumb until you have seen the day when honor shall be given back to your dear children!"

This is why, dear Lucie, I come to cry to you always, to you, as to all, "Courage!" and more than courage—for will to accomplish! . . . Oh, silently, very silently—for words do not help—but boldly, audaciously to march straight onward to the end—the entire truth, the light upon this awful drama, in one word, all the honor of our name! Means? They must all be employed, of whatever nature they may be—anything that the mind can suggest to obtain the solution of this enigma.

The object is everything; that alone is immutable. I wish our children to enter upon life with heads proudly erect. I wish to animate you with my supreme desire. I wish to see you succeed, and it will be full time, I swear to you!

I hope that you may soon be able to tell me something certain, something positive, oh, for both of us, my dear Lucie! I cannot write to you at greater length, nor speak to you of anything else except my great and deep affection for you. My head is too tired by this bitter discipline, the most terrible, the most cruel that human brain can endure.

Our dear little Pierre asks me to write to him. Ah, I am not strong enough! Each word wrings a sob from my throat and I am obliged to resist with all my strength in order to be with him on the day when they give us back our honor.

Take him in your arms for me, as well as our dear little Jeanne.

Oh, my precious children! . . . Draw from them your invincible courage.

I embrace you with all the forces of my being, as I love you.

ALFRED.

Embrace your dear parents, all the family for me; my health is good.

I received from you at the beginning of the month a dozen packages of provisions and some cardigans. I thank you for your touching care for me. I have not yet received any of the reviews and the books you announced in your letters of September, December, and January; not one of them has yet arrived at Cayenne. Please send the things so that they may come by parcels post. Either address them to me directly, care of the Director of the Penitentiary Service at Cayenne, or else have them addressed to me from the Ministry, at your own expense.

---

26 March, 1896, evening.

Dear Lucie:

Before sending you the letter that I had written, I reread, perhaps for the hundredth time, your dear letters, for you can imagine what my long days and nights are like, when, my arms crossed, I am alone with my thoughts, without anything to read, sustaining myself only by the force of duty, so that I may uphold you so that I may see, at last, the day when our honor is given back to us. You ask me to await calmly the day when you can announce to me the discovery of the truth.

Ask me to wait as long as I have the strength; but with calmness? Oh, no! When they have torn, all-living, the heart from my breast, when I feel myself struck in my most precious possession, in you and my children, when my heart groans with agony night and day, without one hour of rest, when for eighteen months I have lived in a frightful nightmare!

But, then, that which I desire with a ferocious determination, that which has made me bear everything, that which has made me live, is not that you should protest my innocence by your words, but that you should march, that you all should march, straight forward, no matter by what means, to the conquest of the truth, to the laying bare in the full light of day this dark story . . . in a word, to the recovery of our whole honor.

These are the words I spoke to you before my departure—already more than a year ago . . . and, alas! it is not that I would reproach you; but it seems to me that you are very long on this supreme mission, for it is not living to live without honor.

And in my long nights of torture, suffering this martyrdom, how often have I told myself, "Ah, how I should have solved the enigma of this horrible drama—by any means, no matter what, even had I been forced to put the knife to the throats of the wretched accomplices, however well hidden they might have been, of the vile criminal!" And more often still have I cried to myself, "Will there be no one, then, with enough heart and soul or clever enough to tear the truth from them, and to bring to an end this fearful martyrdom of a man and of two families?" Ah, I know that these are only the dreams of one who suffers horribly! But what would you? All that is too horrible, too atrocious! It leads astray my reason, my faith in loyalty and rectitude, for there is a moral law that is above all things, above passion and hatred; it is the law that demands the truth always and in all things. And then when my thoughts turn back upon my past, upon my whole life, and then to see myself where I am now! Oh, then it is horrible! black night closes in upon my soul, and I long to shut my eyes, to think no more. It is in my thought of you, of our dear children, in my wish to see the end of this horrible drama that I find again the energy to live, to hold myself erect. These are my thoughts, these are my dreams, my dear and good Lucie, and it is in answer to your question that I have thus laid bare my soul. Know, then, that I suffer with you, that I live in your life, that our mental and moral tortures are the same, that they can have but one end—full light upon this sinister affair. Let us press on, then, toward this supreme end, active in every day, in every hour, with ferocious and unconquerable will, the conviction that overturns all obstacles. It is our honor that has been torn from us, and we must regain it. And now I am going to bed to try to rest my brain a little, or rather to try to dream of you and of our dear children. The 5th of April Pierre will be five years old. Be sure that on that day all my heart, all my thoughts, my tears, alas! also will have been of him, of you. And I close in wishing that you may soon announce to me the end of this infernal torture, and by embracing you with all my strength, as I love you.

Your devoted
ALFRED.

LETTERS OF AN INNOCENT MAN

5 April, 1896.

My dear Lucie:

I have just received your dear letters of February, also those of the family. In your turn, my dear wife, you have been subjected to the atrocious anguish of waiting for tidings! . . . I have known this anguish; I have known many others; I have seen things that are deceiving to the human consciousness. . . . Well, I say again, what matters it? Your children are there, they live. We have given them life, we must restore their honor to them. It is necessary to go straight forward to the end, our eyes fixed upon one single object—to go forward with an unconquerable will, with the courage given by the knowledge of an absolute necessity. I told you in one of my letters that each day brings with it its anguish. It is true. When the evening comes, after a struggle of every instant against the turmoil of my brain, against the overthrow of my reason, against the revolts of my heart, then I have a cerebral and nervous depression, and I long to close my eyes to see no more, to think no more, to suffer no more. Then I have to make a violent effort of the will to drive away the ideas that drag me down, to bring back the thought of you, the thought of our adored children, and to say to myself again, "However horrible your martyrdom may be, you must be able to die in peace, knowing that you leave to your children a proud and honored name." If I recall this to you, it is simply to tell you again what effort of my will I put forth in a single day because it concerns the honor of our name, the name of our children; that this same determination should animate you all. I want to tell you also what I suffer from your torture, from that of you all, what I suffer for our children, and that then at all hours of the day and night I cry to you and to all of you, in the agony of my grief, " March on to the conquest of the truth, boldly, like honest and valiant people, to whom honor is everything."

Ah, the means! Little do I care for means. They must be found, when one knows what one wants, and when it is one's right and one's duty to want it.

This voice you should hear at every moment, across all space; it should animate your souls.

I repeat myself ever, dear Lucie; it is because but one thought, one will gives me strength to endure everything.

I am neither patient nor resigned, be sure of that. I long for the light, the truth, our honor throughout all France, with all the fibres of my being; and this supreme desire ought to inspire in you—in you, as in all the others—all courage, all daring, so that at last we may escape from a situation as infamous as it is undeserved.

You have no mercy and no favor to ask of any one. You wish the light, and that you must obtain.

The more the physical strength decreases—for the nerves end by becoming absolutely shattered by so many appalling shocks—the more the energies should increase.

Never, never, never—and this is the cry from the depths of my soul—can a man resign himself to dishonor when he has not deserved it.

To-day our dear little Pierre is five years old. All my heart, all my thoughts go out to him, to you, to our dear children. All my being quivers with sorrow.

What can I add, my dear Lucie? My affection for you, for our children, you know it. It has kept me alive; it has made me endure what otherwise I should never have accepted; it gives me the force still to endure all.

You say that we are approaching the end of our sufferings. I wish it with all my strength; for never have human beings suffered like this. I wrote you a long letter, ten days ago, by the French mail.

I embrace you, as I love you, with all my strength, and also our children.

Your devoted
ALFRED.

I received some days ago the reviews and books that you sent in November. Their tardy arrival may be traced to the fact that they were sent by freight—that is to say, by sailing vessels. I find a little solace in them. But my brain is so shaken, so fatigued, by all these appalling shocks that I cannot fix my mind upon anything. The other parcels you have sent will reach me some day.

Embrace your dear parents, and all of our family for me. I wrote to them by the French mail.

---

26 April, 1896.

My dear Lucie:

In the long and atrocious days of which all these months are made, I have read and re-read your dear letters of February. My heart has bled with the anguish to which you have been subjected during these long months, and of which each word in your letters bears the trace. I could feel how you restrained the shivers of your being, how you held back the overflowing volume of your grief, and in an effort of your loving and devoted heart you found the strength to cry again to me, "Oh, I am strong!"

Yes, be strong, for strength is needed.

One of these nights I dreamed of you, of our children, of our torture, compared with which death would be sweet, and in my agony I cried out in my sleep.

My suffering is at times so strong that I would tear my skin from my flesh, to forget in physical pain this too violent torture of soul. I arise in the morning with the dread of the long hours of the day, alone, for so long, with the horrors of my brain; I lie down at night with the fear of the sleepless hours. You ask me to speak to you at length of myself, of my health. You must realize that after the tortures to which I have been subjected, supporting the atrocious life of the present, a life that never leaves me a moment of rest, day or night, my health cannot be brilliant. My body is broken, my nerves are sick, my brain is crushed, say, simply, that I still hold myself erect in the absolute sense of the word only because I resolved to, so as to see with you and our children the day when honor shall be returned to us.

You ask yourself sometimes, in your hours of calmness, why we have been thus tried. . . . I ask it of myself at every instant, and I find no answer.

We deceived each other mutually, dear Lucie, by alternately recommending each other to be calm and to be patient. Our love tries in vain to hide from each other the thoughts that agitate our hearts.

My anguish when I write to you, the heart quivering with pain and fever, tells me too clearly what you feel when you write to me.

No, let us tell each other simply that if we still live with torn and panting hearts, with our souls shivering with anguish, it is because there is a supreme object to be attained, cost what it may—the full honor of our name, that of our children—and that right speedily, for sensitive people cannot live in a situation whose every moment is a torture.

Very often I have wished to speak to you at length of our children—I cannot. A dull, bitter anger floods my heart at the thought of these dear little creatures, struck through their father, who is innocent of a crime so abominable. . . . My throat contracts, my sobs choke me, my hands are wrung with grief at not being able to do anything for them, for you . . . to struggle to keep from dying in such a situation, and for so long.

So I can only repeat to you, dear Lucie, " Courage, and determination, and action, also, for human strength has a limit."

I wrote you long letters by the last mail; I wrote also to your dear parents, to my brothers and sisters. I hope that these letters will still more embolden your courage, the courage of every one of you, that they will animate your souls with the fire that consumes my own soul—the fire that gives me the strength to still stand erect.

You tell me that you have good reasons for believing that this atrocious situation is not to be of long duration. Ah, I wish with all my soul that this time your hope may not be deceived, that you may soon announce to me something certain, positive; for truly this is suffering too hard to bear!

What can I add, dear Lucie? The hours are all alike in their atrocity for me; I live only by the thought of you, of our children, in the expectation of a *dénouement*, an escape from a situation which has lasted but too long.

LETTERS OF AN INNOCENT MAN

I embrace you with all my heart, as I love you; also our dear children, and I am waiting now until I shall have the happiness of receiving your dear letters, always so impatiently expected.

Your devoted
ALFRED.

Kisses to all.

May 7, 1896.

My dear Lucie:

A few moments before I received your dear letters I was subjected to an outrage—only a mean, shabby trick —but such things hurt one whose heart has been already so deeply wounded. I have not, alas! the soul of a martyr. To tell you that there are not times when I would be glad to die and end this atrocious life would be to lie. Do not see in this any trace of discouragement. The goal is immutable, it must be attained, and it shall be. But I am a human being as well, undergoing the most appalling of martyrdoms for a man of heart and a sense of honor, bearing it only for you and for our children.

Each time they turn the knife in the wound my heart cries with grief. I wept after this last outrage . . . but enough of that. As I was saying, I have just received your dear letters of March, the letters of all the family, and with all the joy of reading the words you have written, I have always as well that sense of bitter disappointment, which you can well realize, that comes from not yet seeing the end of our tortures. How you must suffer, Lucie! how you all must suffer when you cannot hasten the moment our honor will be restored to us, when the wretches who committed the infamous crime shall be unmasked! I wish that this moment may be near and that it may not be too late.

Thanks for the good news that you give me of the children. It is from the thought of them, from the thought of you, that I draw the strength to resist. You must expect that sufferings, the climate, the situation, have done their work. I have left only my skin, my bones, and my moral energy. I hope that this last will carry me through to the end of our trials. You spoke to me of some supplies that I might ask you for. You know that my material life has always been indifferent to me, to-day more so than ever. I have only asked for books, and unhappily I have still only those you sent me in November.

Please do not send me any more provisions. The sentiment which inspires me to beg this favor may be puerile, but everything you send me is, by regulations, subjected to a most minute examination, and it seems to me each time that they give you a slap in the face, . . . and my heart bleeds and I tremble with pain of it.

No; let us accept the atrocious situation that has been made for us. Do not let us try to alleviate it by any care for the material order, but let us repeat to ourselves that we must find the guilty wretch, that we must get back our honor! March on, then, toward this goal; march on, moved by one common, unchangeable will; try to attain it as quickly as possible and give no care to anything else. I, for my part, shall resist as long as I can, for I want to be there, present on that day of supreme happiness when our honor is given back to us.

Say to yourself, that while the head may bow before some misfortunes, that while commonplace condolences may be received in some situations, when it is a question of honor there can be no consolations, but only a goal to be struggled for so long as we can keep up to have that honor restored to us.

Then, for you, as for all of us, I can only cry from the depths of my soul, *Lift up your hearts!* There must be no recrimination, no complaint, nothing but the unswerving march onward to our end—the wretch or the wretches who are really guilty—and we must attain our end as soon as possible.

As I have already told you, there must not remain one single Frenchman who can doubt our honor.

Kiss our dear children with all your heart for me, and yourself a thousand kisses the most tender, the most affectionate kisses of your devoted

ALFRED.

Embrace your dear parents, all our family and friends for me. In the mail which I have just received I have not found letters from any of my sisters except Henriette. I hope that these dear sisters are not sick from these terrible and continued trials.

---

22 May, 1896.

My dear Lucie:

Your good and most affectionate letters of March have been the dear and sweet companions of my solitude. I have read them and re-read them to recall to me my duty each time that the situation was crushing me with its weight. I have suffered with you, with you all; all the frightful anguish through which you have passed has echoed in my own.

You ask me to write to you, to come and tell you all that is in my crushed and bleeding heart whenever my bitterness is too great for me to bear. Ah, my poor Lucie! If I should do as you bid, I should be writing very often, for I have not one moment of respite. But why should I thus tear your heart? I already do this too often, and after I have thus poured out my woes I always regret it bitterly, for you have already suffered enough, far too much for me. But what would you? It is impossible to break away absolutely from one's *ego,* to stifle always the revolts of one's heart, to be always master of one's sick nerves. My only moment when the tension is relaxed is when I write to you, and then all the accumulated grief of the long month at times goes out into what I write ... And then I feel so profoundly in the very depths of my being all the horror of our situation, as well for you and me as for your dear parents, for all our family, that bursts of anger, quivers of indignation, escape in spite of my efforts; then I cry out in my impatience to see the end of this abominable suffering for us all. I suffer because I am powerless to lighten your atrocious sorrow, because I can only sustain you with all the power of my love, with all the ardor of my soul. Ah, truly yes, dear Lucie, I feel all your anguish when each mail day arrives, and after a long month of waiting, of suffering, and of agony, you cannot yet announce to me the discovery of the guilty wretches, the end of our tortures! And if then I cry out, if at times I roar aloud, if the blood boils in my veins with all this agony, so long drawn out, so undeserved, oh, it is as much for you as for me! For if I had had only myself to think of in my sufferings, long ago I should have put an end to it all, leaving it to the future to be the final judge of everything.

It is from the thought of you, the thought of our

dear children, from my determined resolve to sustain you, to live to see the day when our honor shall be given back to us, that I draw all my strength. When I sink under the united burden of all my woes, when my brain reels, when my heart can bear no more, when I lose all hope, then to myself I murmur three names—yours, those of our dear children—and I nerve myself again against my agony, and not a sound passes my silent lips. To tell the truth, I am physically very weak; it could not be otherwise. But everything is effaced from my mind, hallucinating memories, sufferings, the atrocities of my daily life, before so exalted, so absolute a preoccupation, the thought of our honor, the patrimony of our children. So I come again, as always, to cry to you with all my strength, with all my soul, "Courage, and still courage, to march steadfastly onward to your goal—the unclouded honor of our name"—and to wish for both our sakes that this goal may soon be reached. The dear little letters written by the children always move me deeply, cause me extreme emotion; I often wet them with my tears, but I draw from them also my strength. In all my letters I read that you are raising these dear little children admirably. If I have never spoken of this to you it has been because I knew it, because I knew you.

To speak of my love for you, the love that unites us all, would be useless, would it not? Still, let me tell you again that my thought never leaves you for an instant day or night, that my heart is always near to you, to our children, to you all, ready to sustain you, to animate you with my unconquerable will.

I embrace you with all my strength, with all my heart, and also the dear children, while I wait to receive your good letters, the only rays of sunshine that come to warm my cruelly wounded heart.

Your devoted
ALFRED.

Kisses to your dear parents, to all.

---

5 June, 1896.

My dear Lucie:

I have not yet received your good letters of April, so I have been forced to content myself by re-reading, as I do each day, often many times a day, your good and affectionate letters of March, and from them I have drawn a little calm. I cannot, however, let the English mail leave without coming to gossip a little with you, without drawing near to you.

Oh, I can see you very well in thought from here, my dear and good Lucie, for you do not leave me for a single moment. I know the moments of your crises, when, after some one has given you hope, that hope is again disappointed; when, after a moment of relaxation, of peace, you fall back into a violent despair, asking yourself with anguish when we shall wake from this abominable nightmare in which we have lived so long. And then you write to me, and you find in your splendid soul, in your loving and devoted heart, the strength to hide from me the atrocious tortures, the appalling anguish through which you are passing.

And then I, who feel, who divine all that—I, whose heart is crushed and wounded in its purest sentiments, in its tenderest love, with the blood boiling in my veins, because I feel all the torture heaped upon us, upon our two families—with my very reason in revolt I go and put into my letters the cries of anguish and of impatience that are in my soul; then I suffer through a long month thinking of the emotion you will feel, and I am still more unhappy.

Instead of bringing you, you who are wounded with me in your honor as a wife and a mother, the moral support, the steadfast, energetic, ardent support which you need in the noble mission you must fulfill, I come, at times, to lament, to occupy you with my little sufferings, my petty tortures, with I know not what, to augment your poignant grief. Forgive my weakness—human weakness, alas! all too natural. Words, indeed, are powerless to depict a martyrdom like ours. But it can have but one termination—the discovery of the guilty wretches, absolute, complete rehabilitation, all the honor of our name, the name of our dear children.

So I am again, as always, adding to this letter, which will carry to you the echo of my deep love, the ardent cry of my soul, Courage, still more courage, dear Lucie, to march on to your goal, with a fierce, resolute, unfailing will; and let us hope, for both our sakes, for the sake of our children, that the end may soon be accomplished.

Embrace our dear little ones tenderly for me. I live only in them, in you, and from that source I draw my strength. Kiss your dear parents for me; give my love to all our friends; thank them for their good and most affectionate letters.

I end this letter with regret, and I embrace you hard, "as hard as I can," as our dear little Pierre says.

Your devoted
ALFRED.

LETTERS OF AN INNOCENT MAN

Evening.

I have just received at last the things you sent me, and the books for the months of December, January and February, and I assure you that I had need of them. Yet more fond and ardent kisses for you, for our dear children, for your dear parents, for all our friends; and I end my letter by this ardent cry of my soul: Courage, always and still more courage, my dear and good Lucie.

---

24 July, 1896.

My dear Lucie:

I have not received your letters of May; the last news I have of you dates back three months. You see that sledge-hammer blows are not spared me. I do not want to augment your grief by depicting my own. Besides it is of no importance. Whatever may be our suffering, however appalling may be our martyrdom, our object is unchanging, my dear Lucie—the light, the honor of our name.

I can do no more than repeat to you this cry of my soul: Courage! Courage! Courage! until the end is attained.

As for me, I retain with all my energy whatever strength remains to me. I repress my brain and my heart night and day, for I want to live to see the end of this drama. I hope, for both of us, that the moment is not far distant.

When you receive these few lines your birthday will have passed. I will not dwell upon thoughts so cruel for both of us, but my thoughts could be with you no more that day than on all others.

LETTERS OF AN INNOCENT MAN

I embrace you with all my heart, with all my strength, you and our children.

Your devoted
ALFRED.

---

4 August, 1896.

My dear Lucie:

I have received your letters of May and June all together, with those of the family. I will not tell you of my emotion, after I had waited so long; for we must not give way to such poignant feelings.

I found but two letters from you in the mail for May. I was happy to see that you were settled in the country with the children; perhaps there you may find a little rest, if there can be any rest for us when our honor has not been given back to us.

Yes, dear Lucie, sufferings such as ours, sufferings so undeserved, leave the mind bewildered. But let us speak no more of it; it is one of those things that provoke irresistible indignation.

If I am nervously impatient to see the end of all our tortures; if, under the influence of the revolts of my heart, my letters are pressing, do not doubt that my confidence, like my faith, is absolute. Tell yourself that I have never said "Hope!" I have said, "We must have the whole truth; if not to-day it will be to-morrow or the day after, but this end will be attained—it must be!" Let us shut our eyes to our tortures; let us compress our brains and steel our hearts. Courage, be valiant, dear Lucie; there must not be one minute of weakness or of lassitude. For us, for our children, for our families, we must have light, the honor of our name. I come now, as always, to cry to you, to cry to all, "Lift up your heart! be strong in your determination!"

I wish with all my heart, for both our sakes, for all of us, to learn that this suffering is to have an end.

Embrace our children for me, and for yourself the fondest kisses of your devoted

ALFRED.

Embrace your parents, all our family, for me.

---

24 August, 1896.

Dear Lucie:

I replied at the beginning of the month in a few lines only to your dear letters of May and June. The impression they made upon me after I had waited so long for them was such that I could not write at length. I read and re-read them each day, and it seems to me that thus for a few moments I am near you, that I feel the beating of your heart close to mine; and when I look at this bit of paper on which I write to you, I wish that I could put in it all my soul, all my heart contains for you, for our children, for you all; I wish that I might imprint upon it all the ardor of my soul, all my courage, all my determination.

Believe, dear Lucie, that I have never had a moment of discouragement as to the end to be attained. But yet what impatience devours me to see the end of our atrocious torture!

There are for those who have hearts sorrows so bitter that the pen is powerless to express them. And this grief, equally poignant for us all, I hide it in my breast day and night, and not one complaint escapes from my lips. I accept everything, stifling my heart, my whole being, seeing only our goal.

I wrote to you in the first days of July a letter which must have troubled you, my dear Lucie; I was then a prey to fever; I had not received your letter. Everything came together! And then the human beast in me awakened, and I cried out in my distress and anguish, as if you were not suffering enough already. But I reacted against my own lower nature, I overcame everything, I surmounted my physical as well as my moral being. Since then I have learned that your letters arrived at Cayenne without delay; in consequence of a mistake made in forwarding them, I received them only with your letters of June.

I can only repeat my words, dear Lucie, for you must, as we all must, fix our eager, unswerving gaze upon the supreme object; we must not indulge in one moment of lassitude until the end shall have been attained! The whole truth must be revealed over all France, all the honor of our name, the patrimony of our children.

Embrace the S——s and their dear children for me. Be sure to tell Mathieu that if I do not write to him oftener, it is because I know him too well; I know that his determination will remain as inflexible as ever, until the day when the light shall burst forth. Thanks for the good news of the dear, little ones; thank your dear parents and all the members of our families for their good letters. As for you, my dear Lucie, strong in your conscience, be invincibly energetic and brave. May my profound love, our children, and your duty sustain and reanimate you.

Again I embrace you as I love you, with all my

strength, as I embrace also our dear children. Now I am waiting for your good letters of July.

     Your devoted

          ALFRED.

---

        3 September, 1896.

Dear Lucie:

 They brought me, just now, the mail for July. I found in it only one poor, little letter from you, that of the 14th of July, although you ought to have written oftener and more at length; but no matter.

 What a cry of suffering escapes from all your letters and echoes in my own! Yes, dear Lucie, never have human beings suffered as have you, as have I, and every one of us. The sweat starts from my forehead when I think of it. I have lived only by straining every nerve, by the most powerful effort of the will, by gripping, compressing all my being in a supreme struggle; but emotions break us down; they make every fibre of the being quiver. My hands are wrung with grief for you, for our children, for us all; an immense cry rises to my throat and stifles me. Ah, why am I not alone in the world! What happiness it would be could I lie down in my grave, to think no more, to see no more, to suffer no more! But the moment of weakness, of the derangement of all my being, of awful anguish, has passed, and now I come to tell you, dear Lucie, that above all deaths—for what agony do not I know, as well that of the soul as that of the body, of the brain?—there is honor; that this honor, which is our right, must be restored to us . . . only, human strength has its limits for us all.

 So when you receive this letter, if the situation is not at last shown in its proper light, act as I already told you last year; go yourself, take, if need be, a child by each hand, those two beloved and innocent beings, and take steps to appeal to those who direct the affairs of our country. Speak simply, from your heart, and I am sure that you will find generous souls who will understand how appalling is this martyrdom of a wife, of a mother, and who will put all the means in their power to work to aid you in this noble and holy work, the discovery of the truth, the discovery of the author of this infamous crime. Oh, dear Lucie, listen to me well, and follow my counsels! Remember that you must see but one thing, our object, and strive to attain it; for, oh! I long with all my heart to see, before I succumb to this weight of suffering, honor restored to the name that our dear, adored ones bear. I long to see you again happy, our children, enjoying the happiness that you so merit, my poor and dear Lucie! And as this paper seems to me cold, because I cannot put on it all that my heart contains for you, for our children, I would that I might write to you with my blood; perhaps then I might express myself better. . . .

And although I cannot tell you anything new I continue to talk with you, for the long night is coming, traversed by horrible nightmares, in which I shall see you, our children, my dear brothers and sisters, all those whom we love. You see, dear Lucie, that I tell you everything, that I pour out to you all my sufferings, that I tell you all my thoughts; indeed, in this hour I am incapable of doing otherwise.

And my thought night and day is always the same; my lips breathe forth the same cry; oh, all my blood, drop by drop, for the truth of this appalling mystery!

Pardon the incoherence of this letter. I write to you,

as I have told you, under the influence of a profound emotion, not even trying to assemble my ideas, feeling that I would be incapable of doing it, telling myself with dread that I must pass all of one long month having for my reading only your few poor lines, where you speak to me of the children, where you do not speak to me of yourself, where I shall have nothing to read that speaks of you.

But I am going to try to collect my thoughts. My sufferings are great, like yours, like ours; the hours, the minutes, are atrocious, and they will continue to be so until light, full and entire, shall shine upon the truth. And as I have told you, I am convinced that if you act in person, if you speak from your heart, they will set every means to work to shorten, if possible, the time, for if time is nothing, as far as the object we must reach, which is more important than everything, is concerned, it counts, alas! for us all, for one cannot live and endure such sufferings.

I regret to realize that I must end this letter in which I feel how powerless I am to express the affection that I feel for you, for our children, for all; what I suffer from our atrocious tortures; to make you feel all that is in my heart; the horror of this situation, of this life, a horror that surpasses all that can be imagined, all that the human brain can dream; and, on the other hand, the duty which commands me imperiously, for your sake and for our children's, to go on as far as I shall be able. Think that it will be a month now before I can get one word from you, the only human word that comes to me!

But I must end this prattling, although it eases my pain, for I feel your presence near me in these lines that you are to read, and in ending my letter I cry to you,

"Courage, yet more courage!" for before all things is the honor of the name that our dear children bear. I tell you that this object for which you are striving is immutable. Therefore act as I have said; for the coöperation of generous hearts that you will find—I am sure of it—will realize more speedily the supreme wish that I still cry out, the light of truth upon this sad tragedy, that I may be with our little ones on the day when honor is restored to us! And I add for your own self, for all of us, this ardent and supreme cry of my soul, that rises in the darkness of the night: everything for honor. Let this be our only thought; your sole preoccupation. There must not be one minute of ease.

---

4 September, 1896.

Dear and good Lucie:

I wrote you a letter last night under an impression caused by the mail, the sufferings that we all endure, the pain of having only a few lines from you, for after a long, agonized silence of a whole month, there is now, inevitably, a strong nervous tension. I am as if crazed by grief. I take my head in my two hands, and I ask by what miserable destiny so many human beings are called upon to suffer so.

I feel, too, the need of coming again to talk with you. Perhaps this letter may yet catch the English mail and go with the other.

If I am tired, worn out, if I should tell you the contrary you would not believe me; for to suffer so without respite through all hours of the day and night; to feel intuitively the sufferings of those we love; to see our children, those dear little creatures, for whom I would give, for whom we would give, every drop of blood in our veins, struck down—all that is sometimes too atrocious and the pain is too great to bear. But I am, dear Lucie, neither discouraged nor broken down, believe it well. The more the nerves are strained by all these sufferings, the more the will should become vigorous in its determination to bring the trial to an end. And the only way to end our tortures, the tortures of all of us, is to bring about the discovery of the truth. If I live in a struggle against my body, against my heart, against my brain, fighting against all with a ferocious energy, it is because I wish to be able to die tranquilly, knowing that I leave to my children a pure and honored name; knowing that you are happy. What it is necessary for you to tell yourself, for us all to tell ourselves, is that there can be but one termination for our situation—the light—and then, starting forward with this one word, which outweighs everything, we must smother all that groans in our hearts; we must see only our object and stretch every nerve to attain it; and that soon, for the hours now weigh like lead. We must appeal, as I told you yesterday evening, to all who can help us, to every aid, to all kind hearts, who can help let in the light. I am sure that you will find many, and in the presence of this immense sorrow, the appalling sorrow of a wife and mother, who asks only for the truth, the honor of the name that her children bear, all will be silent that they may see only the supreme object of this work, as noble as it is exalted. Then, dear Lucie, to moan, to lament, to tell each other how we suffer, all that will advance nothing.

Be calm, collected, but gather all your strength, surround yourself with all the advice that can help you to pursue and to attain the object, and let us hope, for your sake, that the time may not be too long in coming. Embrace your parents, our brothers and sisters, and all your family for me.

I embrace you as I love you, more passionately than I ever have done before—with all the strength of my affection, and kiss for me our dear and adored children.

Your devoted

ALFRED.

---

5 o'clock in the morning.

Before I send this letter I must come once more to embrace you with all my soul, with all my strength; to repeat to you that your conscience, your duty, our children, ought to be for you irresistible levers too strong for any human grief to bend.

September, 1896.

Dear and good Lucie:

I wrote to you upon the receipt of the July mail. The nervous strain has been too strong, too violent. I have an irresistible longing to come to talk to you, after this long, agonized silence of a whole month.

Yes, sometimes my pen falls from my hands, and I ask myself what I gain by writing so much. I am dazed by all my suffering, my poor and dear Lucie.

Yes, often, also, I ask myself what I have done that you, whom I love so much, that my poor children, that all of us, should be called to suffer thus; and, truly, I have moments of ferocious despair, of anger also, for I am not a saint. But then I call up, as I have always called up, the thought of you, of the poor little ones, and I evoke that feeling with which I have wished to inspire you, to inspire you all, since the beginning of this sad tragedy—that is, that there is above all our anguish something higher, more exalted. My letter is like a howl of pain, for we are like sorely wounded men whose minds are so worn out with pain, whose bodies are so maddened by long suffering, that the least thing causes their cups, full, too full, of sorrow, to overflow.

But, dear Lucie, to speak forever of our grief is not a remedy for it, it only exasperates it. We must look at things as they are, and we all are horribly unhappy.

Truly the end dominates everything—sufferings, life. I have told you this often and often, for it concerns the honor of our name, the life of our children. This object must be pursued without weakness until it is attained. But the human spirit is formed in such a way that it lives in the impressions of each day, and each day is composed of too many appalling minutes; we have been waiting for so long a time for a happier to-morrow.

It is not with anger, it is not with lamentations, that you must hasten the moment when the truth shall be revealed. Concentrate your courage—and it ought to be great—strong in your conscience, strong in the duty you have to fulfill; look only to your object; look only into your heart of a wife, of a mother, the heart that for so many months has been so horribly crushed and ground.

Oh, dear Lucie, listen to me well, for I have suffered so much, I have borne so many things, that life is profoundly indifferent to me, and I speak to you as from the tomb, from the deep, eternal silence which raises man above all the anxieties of earth. I speak to you as a father, in the name of the duty to your children that you must fulfill. Go to the President of the Republic, to the Ministers, even to those who had me condemned; for if passions, excitements, at times lead astray the most upright minds, the hearts remain always generous and are ready to forget what carried them away before the appalling grief of a wife, of a mother, who wants but one thing—the only thing we ask—the discovery of the truth, the honor of our dear little ones. Speak simply, forget all the little miseries—of what importance are they when compared with the object to be attained? —and I am sure that you will find an army of generous, ardent souls, who will help you to escape from a situation so atrocious, and borne so long that I am yet asking myself how our brains have been able to resist its attacks.

I am speaking to you in perfect calmness in this deep silence, a painful silence, it is true, but it lifts the soul above it all. . . . Act as I beg you to. . . .

See but one thing, my dear and good Lucie, the end which we must attain—the truth—and appeal to all who are just and devoted. . . . Oh, for that! I wish it with all the fibres of my being—to see the day when honor shall be again restored to us!

Courage, then, dear Lucie; I ask it of you with all my heart, with all my soul.

I embrace you as I love you, with all the power of my love, and also our dear, adored children.

Your devoted
ALFRED.

LETTERS OF AN INNOCENT MAN

3 October, 1896.

My dear Lucie:

I have not yet received the mail of August. Notwithstanding, I wish to write you a few words by the English mail, and to send you the echo of my immense love.

I wrote to you last month, and I opened my whole heart to you, told all my thoughts; there is nothing that I can add. I hope that the combined aid that you have the right to ask for will be given you, and I can only hope one thing—that I am soon to learn that light has been let in upon this horrible affair. What I would again say to you is this: that we must not let the terrible acuteness of our sufferings harden our hearts. It is necessary that our name, that we ourselves, should come out of this horrible situation such as we were when they made us go into it

But in the face of such sufferings our courage should be strong, not to recriminate nor to complain, but to ask, to demand, indeed, light on this horrible drama, that he or they whose victims we are be unmasked. But I have spoken to you at length of all this in my last letter; I will not repeat myself.

If I write to you often, and at such length, it is because there is something that I would express better than I do express it. It is that, strong in our consciences, we must lift ourselves high above all this, without moaning, without complaining, like sensitive, honorable people, who are suffering a martyrdom to which they may succumb. We must simply do our duty. If my part of this duty is to stand fast as long as I can, your part of it, the part of you all, is to demand that the light may shine in upon this lugubrious drama, to appeal to all who can aid in bringing about the truth; for truly I doubt that human beings have ever suffered more than we are suffering. I ask myself each day how we have been able to keep alive.

I end this prattle with regret. This moment so short, so fugitive, when I come to chat to you, when I pretend to myself that I am talking with you, that I am telling you all that is in my heart. But alas! I feel too keenly that I eternally repeat myself; for there is only one thought in the bottom of my heart; there is only one cry in my soul: to know the truth of this frightful drama, to see the day when our honor shall be returned to us!

I embrace you as I love you, from the depths of my heart, as I embrace my dear and adored children.

ALFRED.

---

5 October, 1896.

Dear and good Lucie:

I have just received you dear letters of August, as well as letters from all the family, and it is under the profound impression not only of all the sufferings that we all endure, but of the pain that I have caused you by my letter of the 6th of July, that I write to you.

Ah, dear Lucie, how weak the human being is, how he is at times cowardly and egotistical! When I wrote as I did, I was, as I think I told you, at that time a prey to fevers that burned me, body and brain—I whose spirit was already so beaten down, whose tortures were already so great. And then in the profound distress of all my being, when I had need of a friendly hand, of a gentle face, delirious from the fever and from pain, when I did not receive your letter, I had to cry out to you in my misery, for I could cry to no one else.

Afterward I regained possession of myself, and I became again what I had been, what I shall remain to my last breath.

As I told you in my letter of the day before yesterday, strong in our consciences, we must raise ourselves above everything; but with that firm, inflexible determination which will make my innocence shine out before the eyes of all France. Our name must come out of this horrible adventure what it was when they made us enter into it. Our children must enter upon life with heads proudly raised.

As for the advice that I can give you, that I have developed in my preceding letters; you must understand that the only counsels I can give you are those that are suggested by my heart. You are, you all are, better placed, you have better advisers, and you must know better than I could tell you what you have to do.

I wish with you that it may not be long before this atrocious situation is elucidated, that our sufferings, the sufferings of us all, may soon be ended. However that may be, we must have the faith that diminishes all sufferings, surmounts all sorrows, so that in the end we may render to our children a stainless name, a name that is respected.

I embrace you as I love you, with all my strength, with all my heart, and also our dear and adored children.

ALFRED.

LETTERS OF AN INNOCENT MAN

20 October, 1896.

My dear Lucie:

I have written numerous letters to you during these last days, and in them I have once more opened my heart.

What can I add to them? I can hope but one thing; it is that at last they will take pity upon such a martyr, and that I shall learn soon that by the efforts of one or of another light has been let in on this terrible tragedy, in which we have suffered so appallingly and so long.

Ah, yes, dear and good Lucie, for your sake, as for mine, I would that I might hear one good word, a word of peace and consolation, coming to place a little balm upon our hearts, that are so crushed, so tortured.

But what I cannot tell you often enough, my good darling, is how I am suffering for you, for our dear children, for all our family. I had not believed that it was possible to live in such sorrow. Well, I will not linger upon this subject. I can only, as I have told you, wish with you, that by the discovery of the truth we may find ourselves at last in that atmosphere of happiness which we used to enjoy so much; that we may find forgetfulness in our mutual love and in the love of our children.

Waiting for your good letters, I embrace you as I love you, with all my strength; and so, also, I embrace our dear children. Your devoted

Kisses to all. ALFRED.

---

22 November, 1896.

My dear and good Lucie:

I did not write to you at the beginning of the month by the English mail, for I expected each day your letters of September; I have not yet received them. As I told you in my last letter, which dates back, alas! a whole month, I hope that other hearts will feel with us the atrocious sufferings of our long months of martyrdom; this incessant, inexpressible torture of every hour, of every minute—in a word, all the horror of such a crushing moral situation. I hope that other hearts are bringing to your aid an ardent, generous co-operation in the work of laying bare the truth; and I can but hope for both our sakes, my poor darling, and for us all, that I shall soon hear a human word that will be a kind word, a word that will put a soothing balm upon our stinging wounds, make our hearts a little firmer, calm the surges of our brains, so shaken by all these emotions, by all these appalling shocks. I can only, therefore, while I wait for your dear letters, send you the echo of my immense affection, embrace you with all my heart, with all my strength, as I love you, as I embrace also our dear and adored children. Your devoted

ALFRED.

Kisses to your dear parents, to all our brothers and sisters, to all our family.

---

22 December, 1896.

My dear Lucie:

Only a few lines while I wait for your dear letters, to send you the echo of my deep love, to repeat to you always, with all my soul, " Courage and faith," and to embrace you with all my heart, with all my strength, as I love you, as I embrace also our dear children.

Your devoted

ALFRED.

Kisses to all.

LETTERS OF AN INNOCENT MAN

24 December, 1896.

My dear and good Lucie:

I wrote you a few lines only a few days ago. But my thought is always with you, with our children, night and day! I know also all that you suffer, all that you all suffer, and I long to come and talk to you before the arrival of your letters, each month so impatiently awaited.

I also know how it calms the heart only to see the writing of those we love, all of whose sorrows we partake; I know also that in this way it seems that we have with us a part of their very selves, of their hearts, feeling them tremble and throb at our sides. And then I wish that I might render better—not my sufferings, you know them. My heart, like yours, is only a bleeding wound; but what I suffer for you, for our children, how my life is wrapped up in you all! And if I still stand erect, despite the agonies that rend my being—for every impression, even the commonplace, the exterior impressions, produce upon me the effect of a deep wound—it is because you are there, you and our children. I have re-read, as I have always done each month, all the letters that I have from you; they are the companions of my profound solitude, all these letters of you all; and it seems to me as I read them that you have not entirely seized my thought, which is perforce somewhat confused by being scattered among all the letters I have written to you.

I have often told you dreams that could never be carried into effect in real life, crushed by the blows that have rained upon me for more than two years without my ever having understood why they fell, my brain, distraught, searching in vain for the meaning of the horrible dream which has held us all enthralled for so long.

I profit by a moment when my brain is less fatigued to try to lucidly explain my thoughts, the scattered convictions expressed in my different letters. The end, you know it, the light, full and unshrouded, that end shall be attained.

Tell yourself, then, that my confidence and my faith are complete; for, on one hand, I am absolutely certain that this last appeal that I made recently to the Ministry has been heard; that in that quarter everything is to be set in motion to discover the truth. And, on the other hand, I see that you all are wrestling for the honor of our name—that is to say, our very lives—and I see that nothing can turn you from your purpose.

Let me add that the point in question is not the bringing into this horrible affair of either acrimony or bitterness against individuals. We must aim higher.

If at times I have cried out in my grief, it has been because the wounds of the heart are at times too cruel, too burning, for human strength. But if I have made of myself the patient man that I am not, that I never shall be, it is because above all our sufferings there is the one, only object—the honor of our name, the life of our children. This object ought to be your very soul, let come what may. You must be, heroically, invincibly, at the same time a mother and a Frenchwoman.

I repeat it then, my dear Lucie, my confidence and my faith are absolutely alike in the efforts of one and all. I am absolutely certain that light shall be let in, and that is the essential thing—but it will be in a future that we know not.

For, alas! the energies of the heart, the forces of the brain, have their limits in a situation as atrocious as mine. I know, too, what you suffer, and it is appalling.

This is why, often, in the moments of my anguish—for it is not possible to suffer so slowly without cries of agony, having but one wish to express, to be with you and with our children on the day when honor shall be given back to us—I have asked you to take steps to appeal to the Government, to those persons who possess sure, decisive means of investigation—means that they only have the right to employ.

Whatever may come of it, and I think I have clearly expressed my thought, my conviction, I can but repeat to you with all my soul, Confidence and Faith! and wish for you, as for me, as for us all, that the efforts of one or of another may soon be crowned with success and may put an end to this appalling martyrdom of the soul.

I embrace you as I love you, as I embrace also our dear children, from the depths of my heart.

Your devoted   ALFRED.

Kisses to all.

---

4 January, 1897.

My dear Lucie:

I have just received your letters of November, also those of the family. The profound emotion that they cause me is always the same—indescribable.

Your thoughts are mine, my dear Lucie; my thought never leaves you, never leaves our dear children, you all; and when my heart can bear no more, when I am at the end of my strength to resist this martyrdom, that crushes my heart incessantly as the grain is crushed in a mill, that tears all that is most pure, most noble, and most elevated within me, that dries up all the springs of my soul, then I cry to myself, always the same words:

LETTERS OF AN INNOCENT MAN

"However atrocious may be your suffering, march on still, so that you may be able to die at peace, knowing that you leave to your children an honored name, a respected name!"

My heart, you know it, it has not changed. It is the heart of a soldier, indifferent to all physical suffering, who holds honor before, above all else; who has lived, who has resisted this fearful, this incredible, uprooting of everything that makes the Frenchman, the man, of all that makes it possible to live; who has borne it all because he is a father and because he must see to it that honor is restored to the name that his children bear.

I have already written to you at length. I have tried to sum it all up to you, to explain to you why my confidence and my faith are absolute; that my confidence in the efforts of one and all is fully fixed; for believe it, be absolutely certain of it, the appeal that I again made in the name of our children, has revealed to those to whom I appealed a duty which men of heart will never attempt to evade. On the other hand, I know well all the sentiments that animate you all. I know them too well to ever think that there can be one moment of enervation in any one of you as long as the truth remains in darkness.

Then all hearts, all energies, will converge toward the supreme object, running toward it with blind, irresistible force. Cheer up until the beast is run to earth, the author or the authors of this infamous crime. But, alas! as I have already told you, if my confidence is absolute, the energies of the heart, of the brain, have limits when the situation is so appalling, when it has been borne so long. I know, also, what you suffer, and it is horrible.

MADAME ALFRED DREYFUS AND HER CHILDREN
Drawn from life by Paul Renouard

Now, it is not in your power to abridge my martyrdom, our martyrdom. The Government alone possesses means of investigation powerful enough, decisive enough, to do it if it does not wish to see a Frenchman—who asks from his country nothing but justice, the full light, the whole truth of the sad tragedy, who has but one thing more to ask of life—that he may yet see for his dear little ones the day when their honor is restored to them—succumb under the weight of so crushing a fate for an abominable crime that he did not commit.

I am hoping, then, that the Government will lend you its co-operation. Whatever may become of me, I can only repeat to you with all the strength of my soul to have confidence, to be always brave and strong, and embrace you with all my strength, as I love you, as I embrace also our dear, our adored children.

Your devoted

ALFRED.

---

6 *January, 1897.*

My dear Lucie:

Again I feel the need of coming to talk with you, of letting my pen run on a little. The unstable equilibrium that with great difficulty I maintain through a whole month of unheard-of sufferings is broken when I receive your dear letters, always so impatiently awaited; they awake in me a world of sensations, of feelings, that I had kept under during thirty long days, and I ask myself vainly what is the meaning of life when so many human beings are called to suffer thus. And then I have suffered so much in the last months that have just passed, that it is only when I am near you that I can warm my freezing heart. I know, too, my darling, as well as you, that I repeat myself always since the very first day of this sad tragedy; for my thought is like your own, like the thought of you all, like the will that must sustain and inspire us.

And when I come in this way to chat with you for a few moments—oh, such fleeting instants!—in regard to that thought which never leaves me night or day, it seems to me that I live for one short moment with you, that I feel that your heart is groaning with mine, and then I long to press you in my arms, to take your two hands in mine, and to say to you again, "Yes, all this is atrocious; but never should a moment of discouragement enter into your soul any more than it ever enters into mine. Just as I am a Frenchman and a father, so must you be a Frenchwoman and a mother. The name that our dear children bear must be washed free of this horrible stain; there must not remain one single Frenchman who has one doubt of our honor." That is our object, always the same. But, alas! if one can be a stoic in the presence of death, it is difficult to be one before this anguish of every day, confronted by this harrowing thought, the question, when is this horrible nightmare to end, in which we have lived so long—if it can be called living to suffer without respite.

I have lived so long in the deluding expectation of a better day to come, wrestling, not against the weaknesses of the flesh—they leave me indifferent; it may be because I am haunted by other preoccupations—but against the weaknesses of the brain, against the weaknesses of the heart. And then in these moments of horrible distress, of almost insupportable pain, so much greater because it is compressed, contained—I can give absolutely no vent to it—I long to cry to you across the space, "Ah, dear Lucie, hurry to those who direct the affairs of our country, to those whose mission is to defend us, that they may bring to you their active, ardent help, with all the means at their disposal, so that at last light may be thrown upon this sad tragedy, that we may know the truth, the whole truth, the only thing that we ask for."

This, then, in a few words, is what I wish, what I have wished always, and I cannot believe that they will not give it to you. It is the co-operation of all the forces of which the government can dispose, to bring about the discovery of the truth; to cause justice to be rendered to a soldier who suffers a martyrdom that is shared by his dear ones; to put an end as soon as possible to a situation as atrocious as it is intolerable—a situation that no creature with a human heart, a human brain, could support indefinitely.

Therefore, I can only hope, for us all, that this union of efforts, of good will, may bring about its result, and repeat to you always unchangingly, Courage and Faith!

And now I have already stopped talking with you, and it is a tearing of my heart to end my letter. But of what can I speak to you? Of our lives, of our children? Does not the future of a whole family depend upon this one thought that reigns in our hearts? Could there, as you have said so truly, be any remedy for our ills other than full and entire rehabilitation?

But if this object is to be pursued without one minute of weakness, of weariness, until it shall have been attained, oh, dear Lucie! I wish, too, with all my soul, that they may realize all the suffering, all the sorrow, accumulated upon so many human beings, who ask only one thing—the discovery of the truth—and now I must end my letter, but be sure that in every minute of the day or the night my thought, my very heart, is with you, with our dear children, to cry to you, Courage! to cry to you again and always, Courage!

I embrace you as I love you, with all the power of my love, as I embrace also our dear children.

Your devoted   ALFRED.

Kisses to all.

---

20 January, 1897.

My dear and good Lucie:

I wrote to you at length on the arrival of your letters. When a man has borne such suffering and for so long there are times when all that boils within him must escape, as the steam lifts the safety-valve in an overheated boiler.

I have told you that I had an equal confidence in the efforts of one and all. I will not go back to that.

But I have told you, too, that even if my heart never felt one moment of discouragement any more than should yours, or the hearts of any of our family, yet the energies of the heart, of the brain, have their limits in a situation as atrocious as it is incredible; the hours become heavier and heavier, and the very minutes no longer pass by.

I know what you are suffering, too, what you are all suffering, and the thought is horrible.

Truly, you know all this, but if I tell it to you again it is because we must now arise to face the situation; because we must face it bravely, frankly. For on the one hand there can be but one end to our atrocious tortures—the discovery of the truth, all the truth, full and entire rehabilitation. And, then, it is precisely because the task is a laudable one, because we all are suffering from the most cruel pangs that have ever tortured human beings, because, also, in this horrible affair there is a double interest at stake—our personal interest and the interest of our country—it is just because of this, dear Lucie, that it is your duty to appeal to all the forces that the Government has at its command to put an end as soon as possible to this appalling martyrdom. It is a martyrdom that no creature having a human heart, a human brain, could resist indefinitely.

I should like to sum up my thoughts in a few words, . . . but, alas! all that I have borne so long in the vain hope, ever renewed, of a better to-morrow, is at last passing the bounds of human strength.

And then what you have to ask—what they ought certainly to understand—is this, that because human strength has limits, and because the only thing that I ask of my country is the discovery of the truth, the full light, to see, for the sake of my little ones, the day when honor is given back to them, they must set everything in motion, to hasten the moment when the end shall be attained. I am absolutely convinced that they will listen to you, that their hearts will be moved by our immense grief, by this prayer of a Frenchman, a father.

Whatever may become of me, let me repeat to you with all the forces of my soul, Courage and Faith! Let me say again that my thoughts do not leave you for a single moment; that it is the thought of you, of our children, that gives me strength to live through these long and atrocious days; that I embrace you with all my heart, with all my strength, as I love you, as I embrace also our dear and adored children, while I wait for your dear letters, the only ray of happiness that comes to warm my crushed and broken heart.

Your devoted
ALFRED.

---

21 January, 1897.

Dear Lucie:

I wrote to you at length last night. I come again to talk to you. I repeat myself always, alas! I say always the same things; but when one suffers thus, without respite, he must needs open his heart, in spite of himself, to one in whose affection he trusts. And, then, this tension of the brain becomes too excessive, and I ask myself each day how I resist it. When I read over my letters I can see how powerless I am to express our common sorrow and all the sentiments that are in my heart. And, then, because excessive suffering, far from breaking down the soul that is energetic, urges it onward to energetic resolution, because when one has done nothing to deserve it one cannot permit himself to yield, to break down, or to die under even so frightful a fate—because of all this, dear Lucie, I have told you in all my letters, as I told you last night, "Gather around you, around you all, every assistance of every kind heart, so that you may at last see the truth of this sad tragedy, in which we have suffered so appallingly, and for so long a time." It is this that I would repeat to you at every instant in every hour of the day and night.

In a situation so pitiful, so tragic, which human beings cannot support indefinitely, we must rise above all pettiness of mind, above all bitterness of heart, and run straight onward to the end.

LETTERS OF AN INNOCENT MAN

I can, then, only repeat to you always, you must appeal to all devoted and generous spirits; and I have an intimate conviction that you will find such and that they will listen to this cry for help of a Frenchman, of a father, who asks of his country nothing but justice, the discovery of the truth, the honor of his name, the life of his children.

It is this that I tell you in all my letters; it is this that I repeated to you last evening; it is this that I now repeat to you more vehemently then ever. The more the physical forces decrease, the more ought the energies to increase, the will to press on. I can, then, dear Lucie, but wish for you and for me, for all of us, that this united effort may bring about its result.

I embrace you with all the power of my love, and our dear and good children.

Your devoted

ALFRED.

---

5 February, 1897.

Dear and good Lucie:

It is always with the same poignant, profound emotion that I receive your dear letters. Your letters of December have just been given to me.

To tell you of my sufferings—what good would it do?

You must fully realize what they are, accumulated thus without one moment of truce or rest in which I might renew my strength and brace up my heart and my worn-out, disordered brain.

I have told you that I have equal confidence in the efforts of one and all; that, on one hand, I have an absolute conviction that the appeal I again made has been heard, and that, knowing you all as I do, you will not fail in your duty.

What I wish to add is this: We must not bring into this horrible affair either bitterness or acrimony against individuals. To-day I shall repeat it to you as on the first day, above all human passions is our country.

Under the worst sufferings, under the most atrocious abuse and insult, when the human beast awakes ferocious, making reason vacillate under the torrents of blood that burn the eyes, the temples, the whole being, I have thought of death, I have longed for it, often I called to it with all my spirit; but my lips are ever hermetically sealed, because I want to die not only an innocent man, but a good and loyal Frenchman, who never for one single instant has forgotten his duty to his country. Then, as I told you, I think, in my last letters, precisely because the task is laudable; because your means, all your means, are limited by interests other than our own; finally because I may not be long able to resist a situation so atrocious, and when the only thing I ask of my country is the discovery of the truth, that I may see for my dear little ones the day when honor shall be given back to us—it is for all this, dear Lucie, that you must appeal to all the forces that a country, a government, has power over, to seek to put an end as soon as possible to this fearful martyrdom; for be assured my nervous and cerebral exhaustion is great, and it is more than time that I should hear at last a human word that is a kind word. Well, I hope for us all that all these efforts are soon to throw light upon this dark drama and that I am soon to learn something certain, positive; so that at last I may sleep, may rest a little.

But whatever may become of me, I wish to repeat to you with all my soul, Courage and Faith!

I embrace you as I love you, with all the strength of my soul, and our dear little ones.

Your devoted   ALFRED.

Kisses to your dear parents, to all our family.

---

20 February, 1897.

My dear Lucie:

I have written you numerous letters during these last months, and I repeat myself always. But what I would say is that, if sufferings increase, if the revolt against it all becomes almost unendurable, the sentiments that reign in my soul, that should reign in yours, all your souls, are unvarying.

But I shall not write long. Ah, it is not that my thought is not with you, with our children, night and day, since that thought alone makes me live! There is not an instant when, mentally, I do not speak to you; but in the presence of the tragic horror of a situation so appalling, and so long borne, in the presence of the atrocious sufferings of us all, words lose their meaning; there is nothing more to say. There is left only one duty for you to fulfill—a duty that is unvarying, immutable.

Moreover, I have given you all the advice that my heart can suggest.

I can wish only to hear soon a human word, a word that will put a soothing balm upon so deep a wound, that will give new strength to the heart and rest the worn-out brain.

LETTERS OF AN INNOCENT MAN

But whatever may come of it, again I repeat to you always, with all the strength of my soul, Courage! Courage! Our children, your duty, are for you supports that no human suffering should weaken.

I wish, then, simply to send you, while I wait for your dear letters, the echo of my profound love, to embrace you with all my heart, as I love you, and also our dear, adored children.

ALFRED.

My best kisses to your parents, to all our friends. I need not write to them; all our hearts beat in unison.

---

5 March, 1897.

My dear and good Lucie:

I wrote you a few lines the 20th of February while I was waiting for your dear letters, which have not yet reached me. I have just learned that, in consequence of an accident to the machinery, the steamer has not yet arrived at Guiana.

As I told you in my last letter, we know too well, each one of us, the horrible acuteness of our sufferings, to give us any reason to speak of it.

But I would, if it were possible, impregnate this cold and commonplace paper with all that my heart contains for you, for our children. At every instant of the day and of the night you tell yourself that my thought is with them; and that when my heart can bear no more, when the too-full cup overflows, it is in murmuring these three names that are so dear to me, it is in telling myself always, that for their sakes I must live to see the day when honor shall be given back to the name of my children, that I find, at last, the strength to overcome the atrocious nausea, that I find the strength to live.

As to the counsel that I would give you, it never changes.

I have told you everything at length in my numerous letters of January, and it may be summed up in a few words, the co-operation of all the forces of Government to hasten the moment when the truth shall be discovered; to put an end as soon as possible to such a martyrdom.

But whatever may come of it, I want to repeat to you always, that high above all our sufferings, above all our lives, there is a name that must be re-established in all its integrity in the eyes of all France. This sentiment should reign in your soul, in the souls of us all.

I wish only for you, my poor darling, as for me, as for us all, that all hearts may realize with us all the tragic horror of a situation so appalling and borne so long, this terrible torture of human souls, whose hearts are suffering, as under the blows of a hammer, night and day, without truce or rest. I wish for us all that by a powerful union of determined wills the only thing that we have so long asked for may be brought to pass—the whole truth in regard to this sad tragedy, and that I may hear soon one human word coming to put a soothing balm upon so deep a wound.

I embrace you as I love you, with all the force of my affection.

Kiss the dear little ones for me.

Your devoted   ALFRED.

My fondest kisses to your dear parents, to all the family.

LETTERS OF AN INNOCENT MAN

28 March, 1897.

Dear Lucie:

After a long and anxious waiting I have just received a copy of two letters from you written in January. You complain that I do not write more at length. I wrote you numerous letters toward the end of January; perhaps by this time they have reached you.

And then, the sentiments that are in our hearts, and that rule our souls, we know them. Moreover, we have, both of us, drained the cup of all suffering.

You ask me again, dear Lucie, to speak to you at length about my own self. Alas! I cannot. When one suffers so atrociously, when one has to bear such misery of soul, it is impossible to know at night where one will be on the morrow.

You will forgive me if I have not always been a stoic; if often I have made you share my bitter grief, you who had already so much to bear. But sometimes it was too much; and I was absolutely alone.

But to-day, darling, as yesterday, let us put behind us all complaints, all recriminations. Life is nothing! You must triumph over all griefs, whatever they may be, over all sufferings, like a pure, exalted human soul that has a sacred duty to fulfill.

Be invincibly strong and valiant; keep your eyes fixed straight before you, looking to the end—looking neither to the right nor to the left.

Ah, I know well that you, too, are only a human being, . . . but when grief becomes too great, when the trials that the future has in store for you are too hard to bear, then look into the faces of our children, and say to yourself that you must live, that you must be there, to sustain them until the day when our country shall recognize what I have been, what I am.

Moreover, as I have told you, I have bequeathed to those who condemned me a duty in which they will not fail; I am absolutely sure of it.

To speak of the education of the children is needless, isn't it? We have too often, in our long conversations, gone thoroughly over this subject, and our hearts, our feelings, everything, are bound so close together that naturally we agree as to what that education should be; it may be summed up in a word: to make them strong, physically and morally.

I will not dwell too long upon all this, for these thoughts are too sad, and I do not want to be weighed down by them.

But what I wish to repeat to you with all the force of my soul, with a voice that you should always hear, is "Courage, courage!" Your patience, your resolution, that of all of us, should never tire until the truth, full and absolute, shall have been revealed and recognized.

I cannot fill my letters full enough of all the love that my heart contains for you, for you all.

If I have been able to resist until now so much agony of soul, all mental misery and trial, it is because I have drawn strength from the thought of you and of the children.

I am now hoping that your letters of April may reach me soon, and that I shall not have to suffer so long a delay before receiving them.

I will end this letter by taking you in my arms and pressing you to my heart.

I embrace you with all the strength of my love, and

LETTERS OF AN INNOCENT MAN

I repeat to you always and still again: "Courage, courage!"

A thousand kisses to our dear children.

Your devoted

ALFRED.

And for all of you, whatever may come, whatever may become of me, this earnest cry, the invincible cry of my soul: "*Lift up your hearts!* Life is nothing, honor is all!" And for you, all the tenderness of my heart.

---

24 April, 1897.

Dear Lucie:

I want to talk with you while I wait for your dear letters, not to speak of myself, but to tell you always the same words, which ought to sustain your unalterable courage; and then, too, it is a human weakness, that is excusable enough, to get a little warmth for my tortured heart near yours, alas! not less sad than mine.

I have read over your letters of February in which you are astonished, in which you almost make excuses because at times cries of grief, of revolt, escape from your heart. Do not make excuses for them; they are only too legitimate. In this long agony of thought to which I am subjected, be sure that I know them, those very griefs.

Yes, truly, all this is appalling. No human word can express such sorrows, and sometimes I have wanted to shriek out, so inexpressible is such anguish. I also have terrible moments, atrocious moments, the more appalling because they are restrained, because never a complaint escapes my silent lips, when reason is submerged, and all that is in me is agonized, cries out in revolt. I have told you that for a long time in my dreams I have often thought, "Ah, yes, to hold one of those miserable accomplices of the author of that crime between my hands for a few minutes—and were I compelled to tear his skin from him shred by shred, I should make him confess this vile machination against our country; but all that, sorrows and thoughts, they are only sentiments, they are only dreams, and it is the reality that we must see. And the reality is this, always the same: it is that in this horrible affair there is a double interest at stake—that of the country, our own—and one is as sacred as the other.

It is for this reason that I will not try to understand, I will not try to know, why they have made me thus fall under the weight of all these tortures. My life belongs to my country, to-day as yesterday it is hers, let her take it; but if my life belongs to her, her imprescriptible duty is to see to it that the light, full and entire, shall shine upon this horrible drama, for my honor does not belong to the country, it is the patrimony of our children, of our families.

So now, dear Lucie, I shall repeat always, to you and to all, stifle your hearts, compress your brains; as for you, you must be heroically, invincibly, at once a mother and a Frenchwoman.

Now, darling, I cannot speak to you of myself any more. If you could know all that I have been subjected to, all that I have borne, your soul would shiver with horror, and yet I am a human being who has a heart, a heart swollen to bursting, and I need, I thirst for rest. Oh, think how many appalling minutes are contained in one day of twenty-four hours, in the most complete, the most absolute idleness, with nothing to do but twirl my thumbs—alone with my thoughts!

If I have been able to resist so many torments until now it is because I have often called up the thought of you, of the children, of you all, and then I realized what you suffer, what you all suffer.

Then, darling, accept everything, whatever may come; bear it, suffer in silence, like a true human soul, exalted and very proud—the soul of a mother who is resolved to see the name she bears, the name her children bear, cleansed from this horrible stain. Then to you, as to you all, again and always, "Courage, courage!"

You must kiss the dear children for me and tell them how dearly I love them.

And you must also kiss your dear brothers and sisters, and all my family for me.

And for yourself, for our dear children, all that my heart contains of unfailing love.

ALFRED.

---

4 May, 1897.

Dear and good Lucie:

I have just received your letters of March, with those of the family, and it is always with the same poignant emotion, with the same sorrow that I read your words, that I read the letters from you all, so deeply wounded are all our hearts, so torn by all our sufferings.

I have already written to you, some days ago, when I was waiting for your dear letters, and I told you that I did not wish to know or to understand why I had been thus crushed, under every punishment.

But if, in the strength of my conscience, in the consciousness of my duty, I have been enabled to raise myself above everything, ever and always to stifle my heart, to choke down every revolt of my being, it does not follow that my heart has not deeply suffered, that it is not, alas! torn to shreds. But I told you, too, that never has the temptation to yield to discouragement entered my soul, nor should it ever again enter into yours, nor into the soul of any one of you. Yes, it is atrocious to suffer thus; yes, all this is appalling, and it is enough to shake every belief in all that makes life noble and beautiful; . . . but to-day there can be no consolation for any one of us other than the discovery of the truth, the full light.

Whatever, then, may be your pain, however bitter the grief of every one of you, tell yourself that you have a sacred duty to accomplish, and that nothing must turn you from it; and this duty is to re-establish a name, in all its integrity, in the eyes of all France.

Now, to tell you all that my heart contains for you, for our children, for you all, is unnecessary, isn't it?

In happiness we do not begin to perceive all the depth, all the powerful tenderness that the deep recesses of the heart hold for the beloved. We need misfortune, the sense of the sufferings endured by those for whom we would give our last drop of blood, to understand its force, to grasp the tremendous power of it. If you knew how often in the moments of my anguish I have called to my assistance the thought of you, of our children, to force me to live on, to accept what I should never have accepted but for the thought of duty.

And this always brings me back to it, my darling; do your duty, heroically, invincibly, as a human soul, exalted and very proud, as a mother who is determined that the name she bears, the name her children bear, shall be cleansed of this horrible stain.

Say to yourself, then, as to every one, always and again, "Courage, courage!" I cannot tell you of myself; I gave you my reasons in my former letter. I want only to end these few lines by embracing you with all my heart, with all my strength, as I embrace also our dear children.

Your devoted
ALFRED.

Thank your dear parents, all our family, for their letters, so full of profound tenderness and with grief not less profound.

Why should I write to them? To speak of myself, of our sufferings? We all know each other too well not to know both the intense love that unites us and the deep grief that fills our souls. But for all, unchangingly, unalterable, steadfast courage! As ——— has said so truly: there is an object to attain, and in the thought of that object we must forget all present griefs, whatsoever they be!

———

20 May, 1897.

My dear Lucie:

Very often I have taken my pen to talk with you—to unburden my bruised and bleeding heart, as in the presence of yours—but each time I did so the cries of our common sorrow burst out in spite of me.

And of what good is it to cry out? In the presence of such martyrdom, in the presence of such sufferings, I must be silent. So what I will repeat to you is simply this: it is the invariable, the ever-ardent, persistent cry of my soul, "Courage, courage!" When you consider the end we are to attain you should count neither time nor sufferings. We must wait with confidence until it shall be attained.

I embrace you, as I love you, with all the power of my love, and so also I embrace our dear children.

Your devoted

ALFRED.

My best kisses to your dear parents, to all of our family.

---

5 July, 1897.

My dear and good Lucie:

I have just received your letters of April with those of May, and with all the letters of the family; with all the strength of my soul I add mine to your most hearty good wishes for Marie's happiness. Kiss her for me and tell her, too, that I found some tears—I who no longer know how to weep—in thinking of her joy that is mingled with so much suffering.

I wish with all the strength of my soul, for you, my poor darling, that the end of this terrible martyrdom may be near, and if one who has suffered so deeply can still pray, I join my hands in one last prayer that I address to all those to whom I have appealed, that they may bring you a co-operation more ardent, more generous than ever in the work of discovering the truth. Moreover, I am certain that you have this co-operation, have it fully, ungrudgingly, . . . and I hope with all that my heart contains of tenderness for you, of affection for our children, that all these efforts may soon bring about their result.

As for me, dear and good Lucie, I who for you would have given with all my heart, with all my soul, every drop of my blood to relieve one pain, to spare you one sorrow, . . . I have been able to do nothing but remain alive for so long and through so many tortures. I have done it for you, for our children.

But I must repeat to you always, "Courage, courage!" Our children are the future; it is their life that we must assure. And I wish to end these few lines by expressing once more the two sentiments that reign in my heart. First, I want to send you all my tenderness, all my deep love, for you, for our children, for your dear parents, for my dear brothers and sisters. I want to take you in my arms again, to press you again to my heart with all the strength that remains to me, with all the power of my love. And then the second sentiment is this: to repeat to you always to be grand, to be strong, whatever may happen, whatever may be the trials that the future may still have in store for you, to think ever and again of our dear children, who are the future, the children of whom you must be the unfailing guard and stay, until the day when the truth shall be revealed.

And then I want to tell you once again the last prayer of a man who has been subjected to the most terrible of martyrdoms, a man who had always and in all places done his duty; it is that they may give you a kind word, a helping hand, an energetic and powerful aid, that nothing can weary in the discovery of the truth.

All my being, all my thoughts, my very heart, spring forward in a supreme effort toward you, toward our dear children, toward your dear parents, toward all those whom I love, while I wish with all the strength of my soul that a future may be near which will bring to you all a rest of the mind, a calmness, a tranquillity, all the happiness you yourself so well deserve, that you all so well deserve.

Then, dear and good Lucie, always, and still always, Courage!

I embrace you as I love you, as I embrace also our dear and adored children, your dear parents, all our family.   Your devoted

ALFRED.

---

22 July, 1897.

My dear Lucie:

A few lines only, while I await your dear letters.

I suffer too much for you, for our children, for you all. I know too well what are your tortures for me to be able to tell you of myself.

Poor love, did you, too, deserve to bear a martyrdom like this? My heart breaks; my brain bursts its bounds as I think of all the sorrow heaped upon you all—sorrow so unending, so unmerited!

I have again made passionate appeals for you, for our children. I am sure that the co-operation which will be given you will be more active, more ardent, than ever. In my long nights of suffering, when my thought comes back constantly to you, to our children, I often join my hands in a silent prayer into which I put my whole heart, that the appalling suffering of so many innocent victims may soon be ended.

However it may be, dear Lucie, I want to repeat to

you always, as long as I shall have a breath of life, "Courage, courage!" Our children, your duty, are for you safeguards that nothing should displace, that no human grief should weaken.

I want, in ending, to impregnate as well as I can these few lines with all that my heart contains for you, for our dear children, for your dear parents, for you all, to tell you still that night and day my thoughts, all my very being, springs forward toward them, toward you, and it is due to that alone that I live. I want to take you in my arms and hold you to my heart with all the power of my love, to embrace thus also our dear children, as I love you.

Your devoted
ALFRED.

A thousand kisses to your dear parents; again my most profound wishes of happiness for our dear Marie, and many kisses for my brothers and sisters; and to all, without exception, whatever may be their suffering, whatever may be their fearful grief, always courage!

---

10 August, 1897.

Dear Lucie:

I have just at this instant received your three letters of the month of June and all the letters from the family, and it is under the impression, always keen, always poignant, that so many sweet souvenirs evoke in me, so many appalling sufferings also, that I will answer.

I will tell you once more, first all my profound affection, all my immense tenderness, all my admiration, for your noble character; then I will open all my soul to you, and I will tell you your duty, your right, that right that you should renounce only with your life. And this right, this duty, that is equally imprescriptible for my country as for you, is to will it that the light shall shine full and entire upon this horrible drama; it is to will without weakening, without boasting, but with indomitable energy, that our name, the name that our dear children bear, shall be washed free from this horrible stain.

And this object, this end, you, Lucie, you all should attain it, like good and valiant French men and women who are suffering martyrdom, but not one of whom, no matter what bitter outrages he has suffered, has ever forgotten his duty to his country for one single instant. And the day when the light shall shine, when the whole truth shall be revealed—as it must be, for neither time, patience, nor effort of the will should be counted in working for such an end—ah, well! if I am no longer with you, it will be for you to wash my name from this new outrage, so undeserved, that nothing has ever justified; and I repeat it, whatever may have been my sufferings, however atrocious may have been the tortures inflicted upon me—tortures that I cannot forget, tortures that can be excused only by the passions that sometimes lead men astray—I have never forgotten that far above men, far above their passions, far above their errors, is our country. It is she that will be my final judge.

To be an honest man does not wholly consist in being incapable of stealing a hundred sous from the pocket of a neighbor; to be an honest man, I say, is to be able always to see one's reflection in that mirror that forgets nothing, that sees everything, that knows everything;

to be able to see one's self, in a word, in one's conscience with the certitude of having always and everywhere done one's duty. That certitude I have.

Then, dear and good Lucie, do your duty bravely, pitilessly, as a good and valiant Frenchwoman who is suffering martyrdom, but who is resolved that the name she bears, the name that her children bear, shall be cleansed from this horrible stain. The light must break out, it must shine in all its brilliancy. The limitations of time should no longer be anything to you.

Indeed, I know too well that the sentiments that animate me are cherished by you all; they are common to all of us, to your dear family as to my own.

I cannot speak to you of the children; besides, I know you too well to doubt for one single instant the manner in which you will bring them up. Never leave them; be with them always, heart and soul; listen to them always, however importunate may be their questions.

As I have often told you, to educate children is not merely to assure their material life, nor even their intellectual life, but it is also to assure to them the support that they should find in their parents, the confidence with which the latter should inspire them, the certainty that they should always have that there is one place where they can unburden their hearts, where they can forget their pains, their sorrows, no matter how little, how trivial they may sometimes appear.

In these last lines I would put once more all my deep love for you, for our dear children, for your dear parents, for you all, all those whom I love from the bottom of my heart, for all the friends whose thoughts for me I divine, whose unalterable devotion I know; and I would say to you again and again, Courage, courage!

I would tell you that nothing should shake your will; that high above my life hovers the one supreme care— the honor of my name, of the name you bear, the name our children bear.

I would embrace you with the ardent fire that animates my soul, the fire that is to be extinguished only with my life.

I embrace you from the depths of my heart, with all my strength, and so also I embrace my dear, my adored children.   Your devoted

ALFRED.

A thousand kisses for the dear children now and always. All my wishes of happiness for Marie and her dear husband; and as many kisses for all my dear brothers and sisters, for Lucie and Henri.

---

4 September, 1897.

Dear Lucie :

I have just received your letters of July. You tell me again that you have the certainty that the full light of day is soon to shine; this certainty is in my soul; it is inspired by the right that every man has to demand it, to will that he shall have it when he demands but one thing—the truth.

As long as I shall have the strength to live in a situation as inhuman as it is undeserved, I shall continue to write to you, to inspire you by my indomitable will.

Indeed, the last letters I wrote to you are my moral will and testament. I spoke to you in them first of all of our love. I confessed to you also my physical and cerebral breaking down, but I spoke to you not less energetically of your duty, the duty of you all.

LETTERS OF AN INNOCENT MAN

This grandeur of soul that you all have shown equally —let there be no illusion about this—this grandeur of soul should be accompanied neither by weakness nor by boasting. On the contrary, it should ally itself to a determination each day more resolute, a determination that strengthens with each hour of the day, to march on toward the goal—the discovery of the truth, the whole truth, for all France.

Truly, this wound sometimes bleeds too hard, and the heart rises in revolt. Truly, worn out as I am, I often fall under the blows of the sledge-hammer, and then I am no more than a poor human being, full of agony and suffering; but my indomitable soul lifts me up quivering with pain, with energy, with implacable desire for that that is most precious in this world—our honor, the honor of our children, the honor of us all. And then I brace myself anew to cry out to all men the thrilling appeal of a man who asks, who wants, only justice. And then I come to illume in you all the ardent fire that burns in my soul, that shall be extinguished only with my life.

As for me, I live only by my fever; for a long time I have lived on from day to day, proud when I have been able to hold out through a long day of twenty-four hours. I am subjected to the stupid and useless lot of the man in the iron mask, because there is always that same afterthought lingering in the mind, I told you so, frankly, in one of my last letters.

As for you, you must not pay any attention either to what any one says or to what any one thinks. You have your duty to do unflinchingly, and it is incumbent upon you, and to resolve not less unflinchingly, to have your right, the right of justice and of truth. Yes, the light must shine out. I put my thought in a few words; but if there are in this horrible affair other interests than ours—interests that we have never misunderstood—there are also the imprescriptible rights of justice and of truth; there is for us both, for all, the duty, while we respect all these interests, of bringing to an end a situation so atrocious, so unmerited.

I can then but hope for both of us, for all, that our martyrdom is to have an end.

Now what can I say further to express this profound, this immense love for you, for our children, to express my affection for your dear parents, for all our brothers and sisters, for all who suffer this appalling, this long drawn-out martyrdom?

To speak at length of myself, of all my little affairs, is useless. I do it sometimes in spite of myself, for the heart has irresistible revolts; bitterness, do what I will, mounts from my heart to my lips when I see that everything is misunderstood, everything that goes to make life noble and beautiful; and, truly, were it a question of my own self only, long ago would I have gone to search in the peace of the tomb for forgetfulness of all that I have seen, of all that I have heard, of all that I see each day.

I have lived in order to sustain you, to sustain you all, with my indomitable will; for it is no longer a question of my life, it is a question of my honor, of the honor of us all, of the life of our children.

I have borne everything without flinching, without lowering my head; I have stifled my heart; I curb each day the revolts of my being, urging you all again and again to demand the truth, without lassitude as without boasting.

LETTERS OF AN INNOCENT MAN

But I hope for us both, my poor beloved, for us all, that the efforts, either of one or of another, may soon bring about their result; that the day of justice may at last dawn for us all, who have waited for it so long.

Each time I write to you I hardly can lay down my pen, not that I have anything to tell you, . . . but because I am again about to leave you for long days, living only in my thoughts of you, of the children, of you all.

So I will end by embracing you and my dear children, your dear parents, all of our dear brothers and sisters, in pressing you in my arms with all my strength, and repeating with an energy that nothing can weaken, so long as the breath of life is in my body, "Courage, courage and determination!"

A thousand kisses more.

Your devoted

ALFRED.

And for you all, dear parents, and dear brothers and sisters, courage and indomitable will that nothing should shake, that nothing should weaken.

---

2 October, 1897.

My dear Lucie:

I have just received your dear letters of August, also a few from the family.

I wish with you, for you, for us all, that the light of justice may shine at last and that we may at last perceive the end of our martyrdom, that has been as long drawn out as it has been appalling.

Indeed, I have already told you in long letters that

neither my faith nor my courage had been nor shall ever be shaken, for, on one hand, I know that you will all energetically fulfill your duty, and that you will not less inflexibly be resolved to gain your right—the right of justice and of truth; and, on the other hand, I know that if there is any imprescriptible duty devolving upon my country, it is to bring the full light of truth to bear upon this tragic story, to repair this terrible error.

In fact, very often, in so far as my human weakness has permitted me—for if one can be a stoic in the face of death—and I have often called on death from the bottom of my heart—it is difficult to be one through all the minutes of an agony that is as long drawn out as it is undeserved—I have hidden my horrible distress under such tortures to sustain you, to keep you from fainting, from bending in your turn under all the weight of such suffering.

If for several months I have no longer hidden anything from you, it has been because I think that you ought always to be prepared for everything, drawing from the duties which as a mother you must perform heroically, invincibly, the force to bear everything with a firm and valiant heart, with the unshakable determination to wash the infamous stain from the name you bear, that our children bear.

Now, we have had enough of all this, haven't we, darling? Leave their fears, their suspicions, with those who have them. If my soul is always valiant and will remain so to my last breath, everything within me is worn out; my heart swells to bursting not only for past tortures, but to see that you misunderstand me on this point. My brain reels and totters, at the mercy of the least shock, the most petty of events. Besides, as I have told you already, my long letters are too clearly the equally intimate and heartfelt expression of my sentiments and of my immutable will for it to be necessary for me to return to it. They are my moral will and testament.

Therefore, my dear Lucie, for your own sake, for us all, you must always do your duty, be resolved to gain your right—the right of justice and of truth—until the full light shines out; until all France is convinced—and she must be—whether I should live or die; for, like Banquo's ghost, I should come out of my tomb to cry to you all with all my soul, always and again, "Courage, courage!" to remind my country, who thus tortures me, who sacrifices me—I dare to say it, for no human brain could resist so long such an appalling situation, and it is only by a miracle that I have been able to resist until now—to remind my country that she has a duty to fulfill, and that that duty is to throw a refulgent light upon this sad tragedy, to repair this frightful error that has endured for so long.

Therefore, darling, be sure of it, you are to have your day of refulgent glory, of supreme joy; be it by your own efforts, be it by the efforts of our country, who will fulfill all her duty; and if I am not to be there, what would you have, darling? There are victims of state—and truly the situation is too hard to bear—by far too heavy for the length of time that I have borne it—and, well, Pierre will represent me!

I shall not speak of the children; indeed, I already did so at length in my letters of August; and then I know you too well to have any anxiety in regard to them. You will embrace them with all my strength, with all my soul. I must leave you, although it always is a great grief to me to tear away from your presence, so short, so fleeting, is this moment that I pass with you.

I embrace you as I love you, with all my strength, with all the power of my love, as I embrace our dear children, while I repeat to you always, Courage, courage! and while I wish that all this suffering may have at last an end.

Your devoted
ALFRED.

My best kisses to your dear parents, to all of our family; my wishes of condolence to Arthur and to Lucie; I do not feel that I have the courage to write to them.

---

22 October, 1897.

My dear and good Lucie:

Should I listen only to my heart I should write to you at every instant, at every hour in the day; for my thoughts cannot detach themselves from you, from our dear children, from all; but it would be only to repeat the expressions of our common grief, and there are no more words to describe this martyrdom—so long!

In the letters that I have written to you I have expressed my thoughts, my determination, that determination that I know to be your own, that of every one of you, independent of my sufferings, of my life; there have been also in my letters, it is true, cries of sorrow, for when I suffer night and day, even more for you and for our children than for myself, my brain takes fire; and as if there were not enough in my own tortures, the climate at this time of year is sufficient in itself alone. And, indeed, the heart has need to give vent to its anguish, the human being to cry out its distress, its weakness.

But do not let us dwell upon all that. What I wish to tell you is this: you must demand light on this tragic story; you must have the will to pursue inflexibly, without boasting, without passion, but with the unshakable conviction of your rights; with your heart of a wife, of a mother, horribly mutilated and wounded, with an energy and a will increasing each day in proportion to your sufferings.

So, to-day, while I await your dear letters I wish only to embrace you with all my heart, with all my strength, as I love you, as I embrace also our dear children, to hope, as always, that our terrible martyrdom may at last have an end; yes, and to repeat to you always, a thousand and a thousand times, Courage!

A thousand kisses more.

ALFRED.

---

4 November, 1897.

My dear and good Lucie:

I have just at this moment received your letters. Words, my good darling, are powerless to express what poignant emotions the sight of your dear writing awakes in my heart; and, indeed, it is these sentiments of powerful affection that this emotion awakens in me that give me the strength to wait until the supreme day when the truth shall be made clear concerning this sad and terrible drama.

Your letters breathe such a sentiment of confidence that they have brought serenity to my heart, that is suffering so much for you, for our dear children.

LETTERS OF AN INNOCENT MAN

You tell me, poor darling, not to think, not to try to understand. Oh, try to understand! I have never done that; it is impossible for me. But how can I stop my thoughts? All that I can do is, as I have told you, to try to wait for the supreme day of truth.

During the last months I wrote you long letters, in which I poured out my over-burdened heart. What would you? For three years I have seen myself the toy of events to which I am a stranger, having never deviated from the absolute rule of conduct that I had imposed upon myself, that my conscience as a loyal soldier devoted to his country had imposed upon me. Even in spite of yourself the bitterness mounts from the heart to the lips; anger sometimes takes you by the throat and you cry out in pain.

Formerly I swore never to speak of myself, to close my eyes to everything, because for me, as for you, for us all, there can be but one supreme consolation—that of truth, of unshrouded light.

But while my too long sufferings, the appalling situation, the climate, which by its own power alone makes the brain burn—while all this combined has not made me forget a single one of my duties, it has ended by leaving me in a state of cerebral and nervous erethismus that is terrible. I understand thoroughly, too, my good darling, that you cannot give me details. In affairs like this, where grave interests are at stake, silence is necessary, obligatory.

I chatter on to you, though I have nothing to tell you; but all this does me good, it rests my heart and relaxes the tension of my nerves. Truly, my heart often is shrivelled with poignant grief when I think of you, of our children; and then I ask myself what I can have committed upon this earth that those whom I love the most, those for whom I would give my blood, drop by drop, should be tried by such awful agony. But even when the too full cup overflows, it is from the dear thought of you, from the thought of the children—the thought that makes all my being vibrate and tremble, that exalts it to its greatest heights—from this thought that I draw the power to rise from the depths of despair, to send out the thrilling cry of a man who has begged for so long for himself, for those he loves, only for justice and truth—nothing but truth.

I have summed up my resolution clearly, and I know that that determination is your own, that of all of you, and that nothing has ever been able to overcome it.

It is this feeling, associated with all my duties, that has made me live; it is this feeling also that has made me ask once more for you, for you all, every co-operation, a more powerful effort than ever on the part of all in a simple work of justice and of reparation, by rising above all question of individuals, above all passions.

May I still tell you of all my affection? It is needless, is it not? for you know it; but what I wish to tell you again is this, that the other day I re-read all your letters in order that I might pass some of the too long minutes near a loving heart, and an immense sentiment of wonder arose in me for your dignity and your courage. If the trial found in great misfortunes is the touchstone of noble souls, then, oh, my darling, yours is one of the most beautiful and the most noble souls of which it is possible to dream.

You must thank M—— for his few words; all that I can tell him is in your heart as it is in mine.

Then, my darling, always and again, Courage! As

LETTERS OF AN INNOCENT MAN

I told you before my departure from France a long time ago, alas! a very long time, our own selves should be entirely secondary; our children are the future; there must remain no spot upon their name; no cloud must hover, not even the very smallest, over their dear heads. This thought should dominate all else.

I embrace you, as I love you, with all my strength, as also our dear and adored children.

Your devoted   ALFRED.

---

24 November, 1897.

Dear Lucie:

All these months I have written you many long letters, in which my oppressed heart has unburdened itself of all our too long-endured common sorrow. It is impossible to disengage the mind from its *ego* at all times; to rise above the sufferings of every instant. It is impossible that all my being should not quiver, should not cry aloud with anguish at the thought of all you suffer, at the thought of our dear children; and if when I fall I again and again raise myself up, it is to send forth the thrilling appeal for you, for them.

Though my body, my brain, my heart, everything, is worn out, my soul remains intangible, ever ardent, its determination unshaken and strong in the right of every human being to have justice and truth for himself, for those who belong to him.

And the duty of every one is to co-operate in every effort, by every means, toward this single object—justice and reparation; to put an end at last to this appalling and too long-continued martyrdom of so many human creatures.

LETTERS OF AN INNOCENT MAN

I wish, therefore, my good darling, that our terrible tortures may soon be ended.

I have received during the month letters from your dear parents from all our family. I have answered them.

My best kisses to all.

And for you, for our children, all the tenderness of my heart, all my love, all my thoughts, that never leave you for one single instant.

A thousand kisses more.

ALFRED.

---

6 December, 1897.

My dear and good Lucie:

I cannot let the mail leave without writing to you, to repeat to you always, it is true, the same words.

As I have told you, for long months I have lived only by an incredible tension of the nerves, of the will; and it is when I fall under the weight of my sufferings that the thought of you, that of the children, lifts me up quivering with grief, with determination, before that which we hold most precious in this world—our honor, the honor of our children, of us all. And then I send out again the thrilling cries for help, the cries of a man who from the first day of this sad tragedy has begged for nothing but the truth.

Here, then, is a work of justice far above all passions, a duty that devolves upon all, and it must be accomplished. I wish, indeed, for both our sakes, my good darling, that it may be accomplished at last; that our terrible and too long torment may soon be ended.

LETTERS OF AN INNOCENT MAN

I embrace you, as I love you, with all the power of my affection, and our dear, our adored children.

Your devoted

ALFRED.

My best kisses to your dear parents, to all our family.

---

25 December, 1897.

My dear Lucie:

More often than ever I have terrible moments, when my reason totters; this is why I am come to talk to you now, not to speak of myself, but to give you still, as always, counsels as to what I believe you ought to do.

In a situation as tragic as ours, when the question in point is the honor of a family, the life of our children, you must always, my good darling, rise still higher above all; you must put aside from the question all thought of individuals, all irritating subjects, and you must call to your side every aid, every kind heart.

I know better than any one that at times this will be difficult; it is impossible not to feel our wounds; but we must do it. It is not a question of humiliating ourselves nor abasing ourselves; but, on the other hand, we must not throw away our energy in useless outcries; cries are not reasons.

We must simply stand fast, and will it that our right shall be yielded to us, the right of innocence. You must assert your will, energetically, without weakness, with dignity; you must act from your heart of a wife and mother, a heart horribly torn and wounded.

I have suffered too much. I have too often been stunned, felled by their sledge-hammers, to have been able to act in this way myself, although it is the only sane and reasonable line of conduct. And it is just because often I do not know where I am, because the hours weigh so heavily upon me, that I long to pour out my heart to you.

All through this month I have again made numerous and passionate appeals for you, for our children. I want to wish that this appalling martyrdom may have an end; I want to wish that we may come out of this terrible nightmare, in which we have lived so long; but that which I cannot doubt, that which I have not the right to doubt, is that all co-operation is to be given you; that this work of justice and of reparation is to be pursued and accomplished. And now to sum it all up, my darling, what I would tell you in a supreme effort, by which I set my own self totally aside, is that you must sustain your rights energetically, for it is appalling to see so many human beings suffer thus; for we must think of our unhappy children, who are growing up; but we must not bring any passion, we must not allow any irritating questions to enter in, any question of individuals.

I will not speak to you again of my love, when your dear image, that of our children, rises before my eyes, and perhaps there is not a single minute when this vision is not with me; then I feel my heart beat as if to burst, as if it were full of tears repressed.

And a supreme cry rises from my heart in all the minutes of my long days, of my long, sleepless nights; if it is a supreme cry that will be lifted in my last hour, it is also an appeal to all to make one great effort for justice and for truth; that all this ardent and devoted aid may be given you, this aid that all men of heart and honor owe to you.

This appeal, as I have told you, I recently made again, and I cannot doubt that it will be heard, so I will say again to you, Courage!

In these last lines I would now put all my heart, all that it enfolds of love for you, for our children, for all; I would tell you that in my worst moments of anguish it is these thoughts that have saved me, that have made me escape from the tomb for which I had longed, that have made me try once more to do my duty.

I embrace you with all my heart. I want to press you in my arms, as I love you, to ask you to embrace most tenderly our dear and adored children, in a long embrace, and your dear parents, all my dear brothers and sisters.

A thousand kisses more. ALFRED.

---

6 January, 1898.

Dear Lucie:

I have not yet received your letters of October nor your letters of November. The last news I had of you dates back, therefore, to September.

I shall speak to you less than ever of myself, less than ever of our sufferings. No human word can lessen them. I wrote to you some days ago; I was in such a state that I do not remember one word that I said to you.

But if I am totally worn out, body and mind, my soul is always ardent, and I want to come into your presence to speak words that ought to sustain your steadfast courage. I have put our fate, the fate of our children, the fate of innocent creatures who, for more than three years, have been struggling with unbelievable trials, into the hands of the President of the Republic, into the hands of the Minister of War, asking for an end at last to our appalling martyrdom; I have put the defence of our rights into the hands of the Minister of War, whose duty it is to have repaired, at last, this long-enduring and appalling error.

I am waiting impatiently. I want to wish that I may yet have a minute of happiness upon this earth; but what I have no right to doubt for one instant is that justice will be done, that justice will be done you and our children, that you will have your day of supreme happiness.

I repeat to you, then, with all the strength of my soul, "Courage, courage!" I embrace you as I love you, with all my strength, with all the power of my affection, as I embrace our dear and adored children.

ALFRED.

A thousand kisses to your dear parents, to all I love.

---

9 January, 1898.

After long and terrible waiting I have just received, altogether, the mails of October and November.

I need not tell you what indescribable emotion seizes me when I read the letters of those whom I love so much, of those for whom I would give my blood, drop by drop; of those for whose sake I live.

Had I thought, darling, of myself alone, long ago should I have been in my grave; it is the thought of you, the thought of our children, that sustains me, that lifts me up when I am bowed under the weight of so much suffering. I told you in my last letters all that I have done, of all the appeals that I have again made for you and for our children.

If the light that we have awaited for more than three years is not shown now, it will shine forth in a future that we know not.

As I told you in one of my letters, our children are growing; their situation, that of us all, is terrible; the situation I am supporting only by supreme effort is becoming absolutely impossible to bear. That is why I have placed our lot, our children's lot, in the hands of the Minister of War, asking that at last an end may be made of our appalling martyrdom. That is why I have again asked the Minister of War to restore to us our honor.

I await his answer with the greatest impatience, and I am hoping that this appalling torment may have at last an end.

I embrace you, as I love you, with all the power of my love, with all my tenderness, as also I embrace our adored children.

Your devoted ALFRED.

A thousand kisses to your dear parents, to all our family.

---

25 January, 1898.

My dear and good Lucie:

I shall not write to you at length to-day; I suffer too deeply for you and for our children; I feel too keenly all your appalling anguish, your frightful martyrdom. At the very thought of it my heart beats heavily, as if weighed down by unshed tears. No human word could lessen the horror of your anguish.

LETTERS OF AN INNOCENT MAN

I told you in my last letters what I had done; during the last few days I have renewed my appeals; the light we have so long waited for is not yet seen; it will be seen only in a future that no one can foretell. The situation is terrible, terrible for you, for the children, for all. As for me, it is needless for me to tell you what it is.

I have asked the President of the Republic, the Minister of War, and General de Boisdeffre for my rehabilitation, for a new trial. I have put the fate of so many innocent victims, the fate of our children, into their hands; I have entrusted the future of our children to General de Boisdeffre. I await their answer with feverish impatience, with all that remains to me of my strength.

I want to hope that there may yet be one minute of happiness for me upon this earth; but what I have not the right to doubt is that justice shall be done, that justice shall be done to you at least—to you, to our children. I say to you, then, " Courage and Confidence ! "

I embrace you as I love you, with all that my heart contains of deep affection for you, for our adored children, for your dear parents, for all our friends.

A thousand kisses more from your devoted

ALFRED.

---

26 January, 1898.

My dear Lucie:

In the last letters that I wrote to you I told you what I had done; to whom I had entrusted our fate, the fate of our children; what appeals I had sent forth. It is needless to tell you with what anxiety I am awaiting an answer; how heavy the moments have become to me. But my thoughts, day and night, yearn so toward you, toward our children, that I want to write to you again to give you the counsels which I ought to give you.

I have read and re-read all of your letters, and the letters from home, and I believe that for a long time we have been living in a misconception of facts; this misunderstanding comes from different causes (your letters were often enigmas to me)—the absolute secrecy in which I live, the state of my brain, the blows that have been struck me without my understanding them, acts of stupidity that may also have been committed.

But this is the situation as I understand it, and I think that I am not far from the truth. I believe that General de Boisdeffre has never been averse to rendering us justice. We, deeply wounded, ask him to give us light upon this mystery. It has been no more in his power to give us light than it was in ours to procure it for ourselves; it will shine out in a future that no one can foresee.

Some minds have probably been soured; it may be that awkwardnesses have been committed, I cannot tell; all this has envenomed a situation already so atrocious. We must go back to the beginning, and raise ourselves above all our sufferings in order that we may look clearly into our situation.

Well, I, who have been for more than three years the greatest victim, the victim of everything and of every one; I who am here, almost dying of agony, I have just given you the counsels of prudence, of calmness, that I think I ought to give you, oh, without abandoning any of my rights, without weakness, but also without boasting.

LETTERS OF AN INNOCENT MAN

As I have told you, it has not been in the power of General de Boisdeffre any more than it has been in your power to throw light upon this mystery; it will shine in a future that no one can foresee.

Therefore I have simply asked General de Boisdeffre for my rehabilitation; to put an end to our appalling martyrdom, for it is inadmissible that you should undergo such torture, that our children should grow up dishonored by a crime that I could never have committed.

I await the answer to my letters with all the strength that is left to me. I count the hours, I almost count the minutes.

I do not know if his answer will reach me soon; I know still less how I keep alive, so extreme is my cerebral and nervous exhaustion; but if I should succumb before that time comes, if I should faint under the atrocious burden that I have borne so long, I leave it to you, as your absolute duty, to go yourself to General de Boisdeffre, and, after the letters which I wrote to him, the desire which, I am sure of it, is in the bottom of his heart to grant us rehabilitation, when you (*sic*) will have realized that the discovery of the truth is a task that will take a long time, that it is impossible to foresee when it will be accomplished, I have no doubt that he will grant you, immediately, a new trial; that he will at once put an end to a situation as atrocious for you as it is for our children. I hope, too, that over my grave he will bear witness not only to the loyalty of my past conduct, but to the absolute loyalty of my conduct for the last three years, when, under all my sufferings, under all my tortures, I have never forgotten what I have been—a soldier, loyal and devoted to his country. I have accepted all, I have undergone all with closed lips. I do not boast of it, for I have done only my duty, nothing but my duty.

I leave you with regret, for my thoughts are with you, with our children, night and day; for this thought of you is all that keeps me yet alive, and I should like to come and talk like this at every instant of my long days and my long, sleepless nights.

I can only repeat this wish: it is that all this sorrow may have at last an end, that this infernal torture of all the minutes may soon be over; but if you do as I have told you, as it is your duty to do, since I command it, I have no doubt that you shall come to see the end of your appalling martyrdom, the martyrdom of our children.

I embrace you, as I love you, with all the power of my love; I embrace also our dear and adored children.

Your devoted   ALFRED.

Kisses to your dear parents, to all.

---

4 February, 1898.

Dear Lucie:

I have nothing to add to the numerous letters that I have written to you during the past two months; all this medley of confusion may be summed up in a few words: I have appealed to the high justice of the President of the Republic, to that of the Government, in asking for a new trial, for the life of our children, for the end of this appalling martyrdom.

I have made an appeal to the loyalty of the men who caused me to be condemned, to bring about this new trial. I am waiting feverishly, but with confidence, to learn that at last our terrible suffering is to have an end.

I embrace you as I love you, as I embrace our dear children. Your devoted

ALFRED.

A thousand kisses to your dear parents, to all our friends.

---

7 *February, 1898.*

Dear Lucie:

I have just received your dear letters of December, and my heart is breaking; it is rent by the consciousness of so much unmerited suffering. I have told you that the thought of you, of the children, always raises me up, quivering with anguish, with a supreme determination, from the thought of all that we hold most precious in the world—our honor, that of our children—to utter this cry of appeal, that grows more and more thrilling—the cry of a man who asks nothing but justice for himself and those he loves, and who has the right to ask it.

For the last three months, in fever and in delirium, suffering martyrdom night and day for you, for our children, I have addressed appeal on appeal to the Chief of the State, to the Government, to those who caused me to be condemned, to the end that I may obtain justice after all my torment, an end to our terrible martyrdom; and I have not been answered.

To-day I am reiterating my former appeals to the Chief of the State and to the Government, with still more energy, if that could be; for you must be no longer subjected to such a martyrdom; our children must not grow up dishonored; I can no longer agonize in a black hole for an abominable crime that I did not commit. And now I am waiting; I expect each day to hear that the light of truth is to shine for us at last.

I embrace you, as I love you, with all the power of my love; also our dear and adored children.

Your devoted   ALFRED.

A thousand, thousand kisses to your dear parents, to all our family.

---

25 February, 1898.

Dear Lucie:

Our thoughts are in harmony; my thought does not leave you for one single instant day or night; and should I listen only to my heart I should write to you each moment, every hour.

If you are the echo of my sufferings, I am the echo of yours, of the sufferings of you all. I doubt that human beings have ever suffered more. The thought of you, of the children, and my longing always outstretched toward you, toward them, still always give me the strength to compress my bursting brain, to restrain my heart.

I have written you numerous letters in these last months; to add anything to these letters would be superfluous. I have told you all the appeals I have addressed since November last—appeals in which I ask for my rehabilitation, for justice for so many innocent victims.

In one of my last letters I told you that I had just addressed a last appeal to the Government, an appeal more earnest, more energetic than any that I had made before. So I am waiting, expecting day by day to learn that this rehabilitation has taken place, that our tortures, as appalling as they were unmerited, are to end; that the light of justice shines at last. I wish, therefore, to-day only to embrace you with all my strength, with all my heart, as I love you; so, also, I embrace our dear children.

Your devoted

ALFRED.

A thousand, thousand kisses to your dear parents, to all our dear relations, to all our dear brothers and sisters.

---

5 March, 1898.

Dear Lucie:

I have just received your dear letters of January. Your letters are always wonderfully equal in spirit, in feeling, and in elevation of soul. I shall not add anything to the long letters I have written to you during the last three months; the last were perhaps nervous, overflowing with impatience, with pain, with suffering; but all this is too appalling, and there have been responsibilities to establish.

I will not go over and over my thoughts indefinitely. After explaining the details of a situation as tragic as it is undeserved, a situation that has been so long borne by so many victims, I ask and ask again my rehabilitation of the Government, and now I am expecting each day to learn that the light of justice is at last to shine for us.

I embrace you, as I love you, with all the power of my love, as I embrace also our dear children.

My fondest love to all our friends. ALFRED.

APPENDIX

ADDITIONAL LETTERS

A.—1898-99

On September 24, 1898, Dreyfus addressed a piteous letter to the Governor of French Guiana, saying that all his appeals had met with no response. It was at this period that he lost all hope. In early November he received a letter from his wife which, although giving not the slightest intimation of the stirring events in Paris, was in cheerful tone. He thought that it referred to his letter of September 24, and at once became encouraged. After more than two months' silence he wrote to her again. He spoke of the good news contained in his wife's letter, repeated that he was waiting the answer to his petition with confidence, and then he said:

"So when you receive this letter everything will, I think, be finished, and your happiness will be complete. But in these days of relief and felicity which will follow so many days of pain and suffering, I would that my thought, my heart, all that is living in me, which has not left you during those four terrible years, may again reach you, to add, if possible, to your joy until we can at least resume that happy and quiet life to which your natural qualities entitled you, and which you now deserved more than ever owing to the greatness of your soul, to the nobility of your character, to all the most beautiful qualities which a woman can display

APPENDIX

under such tragic circumstances—qualities which suffering has only developed, and which have proved to me that there was no ideal here below to which a woman's soul could not rise, and which she could not surpass. It is in our mutual affection, in that of our dear and beloved children, in the satisfaction of our consciences, and in the feeling that we have done our duty, that we shall forget our long trials. I do not insist. Such emotion is great. I tremble at it; but it is lovely, as it elevates. So until the decisive news of my rehabilitation arrives I am going to live more than ever in thought with you, with all, sharing your common joy."

At length Dreyfus was officially informed of the first decision of the Court of Cassation. Writing to his wife on November 25, he said:

"My dear Lucie:

"In the middle of the month I was told that the petition for the revision of my judgment had been declared acceptable by the Court of Cassation, and was invited to produce my means of defence. I took the necessary measures immediately. My requests were at once transmitted to Paris, and you must have been informed of this some days ago. Events must therefore be moving rapidly. In thought I am night and day, as always, with you, with our children, with all, sharing our joy at seeing the end of this fearful drama approaching rapidly. Words become powerless to describe such deep emotions. . . . According to information which I sent you in the last mail, all will be over in the course of December. Therefore, when these lines reach you I shall be almost on the point of starting for France."

APPENDIX

Here are touching passages from his letter of December 26. After telling his "*chère et bonne* Lucie" —he almost invariably addresses her thus—that, with the exception of the telegram, to which he at once replied, he had not heard from her for two months until he got a letter a few days ago, he went on to explain that if he had for a moment closed his correspondence, this was because he was awaiting the reply to his petition for the revision of his judgment, and should only have repeated himself:

"If my voice had ceased to make itself heard, this would have been because it had forever died away. If I have lived, it has been for my honor, which is my property and the patrimony of our children; it has been for my duty, which I have done everywhere and always; and as it must ever be accomplished when a man has right and justice on his side, without fear of anything or of anybody. When one has behind one a past devoted to duty, a life devoted to honor, when one has never known but one language, that of truth, one is strong, I assure you, and atrocious though fate may have been, one must have a soul lofty enough to dominate it until it bows before one. Let us, therefore, await with confidence the decision of the Supreme Court, as we await with confidence the decision of the new judges before whom this decision will send me. At the same time as your letter I have received a copy of the petition for revision, and of the decree of the Court of Cassation, declaring it acceptable. I read with wonderful emotion the terms of your petition, in which you expressed admirably, as I had already done in mine, the feelings by which I am animated in asking that an end shall be put

APPENDIX

to the punishment of an innocent man—I may add to that, of a noble woman, of her children, of two families, of an innocent man who had always been a loyal soldier, who has not ceased, even in the midst of the horrible sufferings of unmerited chastisement, to declare his love for his native land."

Always confident in the eventual result, Dreyfus wrote on February 8, 1899:

"Although I think, as I told you, that the end of our horrible martyrdom is nigh, what does it matter if there is a little delay? The object is everything, and until the day when I can clasp you in my arms I would have you know my thoughts, which never leave you, which have watched night and day over you and our children. Besides, the letter which I wrote to you on December 26 or 27 was too deep, too adequate an expression of my thoughts, of my invincible will, and of my feelings, for me to add a single word to it."

Pending the receipt of the news of his rehabilitation, he sends his love to all their relatives. The latest letter, dated February 25, runs thus:

"My dear and good Lucie:
"A few lines, as I can only repeat myself, that you may still hear the same words of firmness and dignity until the day when I am informed of the end of this terrible judicial drama. I can well imagine, as you tell me so yourself, what joy you feel in reading my letters. I am

APPENDIX

sure that it is equal to my pleasure in perusing yours. It is a bit of one which reaches the other, pending the blessed moment when we are at last reunited. My thoughts, which have never left you a moment, which have watched night and day over you and our children, are always with you. I very often speak mentally to you, but they are always the same ideas and feelings of which I also find the echo in your letters, as all this is common to us since these same thoughts and sentiments are the common property, the innate basis of all loyal souls and of all honest characters. It is with a reassured and confident mind that I must leave to the high authority of the Court the care of the accomplishment of its noble work of supreme justice. Pending the news of my rehabilitation, I embrace you with all my strength, with all my soul, as I love you and our dear and adored children. Your devoted

"ALFRED."

It was soon after this he wrote the following letter to his little son:

"My dear Pierre:

"I have received your nice little letter. You wish me to write to you. I shall soon do better; I shall soon press you in my arms. Pending this good and sweet moment you will embrace your mamma for me, as well as grandpapa, grandma, little Jeanne, the uncles and aunts, all, in fact. Hearty kisses to you and little Jeanne, from your affectionate father. ALFRED."

This letter, quite exceptionally, does not bear the stamp of the penal administration.

APPENDIX

B.—HIS OWN STATEMENT OF THE CASE

Here is a letter that was received by Maître Demange, the counsel of Dreyfus, from his client, December 31, 1894. It was first made public when sent to M. Sarrien, Minister of Justice, July 11, 1898. In the published copy it was deemed necessary to suppress certain words and phrases:

"Commandant du Paty came to-day, Monday, December 31, 1894, at 5.30 P. M., after the rejection of my appeal, to ask me, on behalf of the Minister, whether I had not, perhaps, been the victim of my imprudence, whether I had not meant merely to lay a bait . . . and had then found myself caught fatally in the trap. I replied that I had never had relations with any agent or attaché, . . . that I had undertaken no such process as baiting, and that I was innocent. He then said to me on his own responsibility that he was himself convinced of my guilt, first from an examination of the handwriting of the document brought up against me, and from the nature of the documents enumerated therein; secondly, from information according to which the disappearance of documents corresponded with my presence on the General Staff; that, finally, a secret agent had declared that a Dreyfus was a spy, . . . without, however, affirming that that Dreyfus was an officer. I asked Commandant du Paty to be confronted with this agent. He replied that it was impossible. Commandant du Paty acknowledged that I had never been suspected before the reception of the incriminating document.

"I then asked him why there had been no surveillance exercised over the officers from the month of February, since Commandant Henry had affirmed at the court-martial that he had been warned at that date that there was a traitor among the officers. Commandant du Paty replied that he knew nothing about that business, that it was not his affair, but Commandant Henry's; that it was difficult to watch all the officers of the General Staff. . . . Then, perceiving that he had said too much, he added: 'We are talking between four walls. If I am questioned on all that I shall deny everything.' I preserved entire calmness, for I wished to know his whole idea. To sum up, he said that I had been condemned because there was a clue indicating that the culprit was an officer and the seized letter came to give precision to that clue. He added, also, that since my arrest the leakage at the Ministry had ceased; that, perhaps, . . . had left the letter about expressly to sacrifice me, in order not to satisfy my demands.

"He then spoke to me of the remarkable expert testimony of M. Bertillon, according to which I had traced my own handwriting and that of my brother in order to be able in case I should be arrested with the letter on me to protest that it was a conspiracy against me. He further intimated that my wife and family were my accomplices—in short, the whole theory of M. Bertillon. At this point, knowing what I wanted to discover, and not wishing to allow him to insult my family as well, I stopped him, saying, 'Enough; I have only one word to say, namely, that I am innocent, and that your duty is to continue your inquiries.' 'If you are really innocent,' he exclaimed, 'you are undergoing the most monstrous martyrdom of all time.' 'I am that martyr,' I replied, 'and I hope the future will prove it to you.'

"To sum up, it results from this conversation:

APPENDIX

1. That there have been leakages at the Ministry. 2. That . . . must have heard, and must have repeated to Commandant Henry, that there was an officer who was a traitor. I do not think he would have invented it of his own accord. 3. That the incriminating letter was taken at . . . From all this I draw the following conclusions, the first certain, the two others possible: First, a spy really exists . . . at the French Ministry, for documents have disappeared. Secondly, perhaps that spy slipped in in an officer's uniform, imitating his handwriting in order to divert suspicion. Thirdly (here four lines and a half are blank). This hypothesis does not exclude the fact No. 1, which seems certain. But the tenor of the letter does not render this third hypothesis very probable. It would be connected rather with the first fact and the second hypothesis—that is to say, the presence of a spy at the Ministry and imitation of my handwriting by that spy, or simply resemblance of handwriting.

"However this may be, it seems to me that if your agent is clever he should be able to unravel this web by laying his nets as well on the . . . side as on the . . . side. This will not prevent the employment of all the other methods I have indicated, for the truth must be discovered. After the departure of Commandant du Paty I wrote the following letter to the Minister: 'I received, by order, the visit of Commandant du Paty, to whom I once more declared that I was innocent, and that I had never even committed an imprudence. I am condemned. I have no favor to ask. But in the name of my honor, which I hope will one day be restored to me, it is my duty to beg you to continue your investigations. When I am gone let the search be kept up; it is the only favor that I solicit.'"

www.ingramcontent.com/pod-product-compliance
Lightning Source LLC
Chambersburg PA
CBHW021354230426
43666CB00006B/517